MOTORCYCLE DREAM RIDE™

*"I wanted to keep reading even when it was time to go to bed.
Thank you for sharing your adventure with us."*

— Sarah in Florida

*"I came to know David by finding and listening to his podcast. Then
came his first book, 'Motorcycle Smarts,' his brainchild. And now his
second book, 'Motorcycle Dream Ride.' I really hope it's not his last.
The appeal of this book isn't just the content, the adventure, the
friendship, but also the style. It's easy to read, though it does have a lot
of details, stats, and real emotions."*

— KP from Earth

"David knows how to tell a story."

— Darren in Fort Worth, Texas

*"An engaging book that I wanted to read right to the end. It inspired
me to get out and do more with my life, so I took a break after a few
chapters to take my motorcycle on a ride. I've been giving ever more
serious consideration to taking some long trips, and this book is
pushing me to finally do it."*

— John in Maryland

*"I loved this book. I started reading it last night and wouldn't go to
bed until I finished it. Now I'm working on answering David's
challenge questions. David has always been a favorite writer of mine."*

— Chris in Wrightstown, Pennsylvania

"Inspiring!"

— Les in Ohio

"I'm not a motorcycle guy, but I thoroughly enjoyed this book! David's humor and easy writing style made it easy to follow along on this great adventure. It's motivating and inspiring and makes you realize that friendship, spending time in nature, and meeting new people are the best parts of life—and that excuses are dream killers. What are you waiting for? Grab a bag of CLIF bars and get out there!"

— Jimmy in Alabama

"This book is about more than motorcycles. It's about friendship and living life to the fullest. David and Mike, thank you for documenting your journey so we could follow along."

— Danielle in Kentucky

"I was so caught up in the story that I could almost feel the wet on rainy days. I'm not a great reader, but I really enjoyed reading this book. It was never a struggle to want to read one more page. Quite the opposite, it was hard to put the book down. I could almost see myself there with Mike and David—a tribute to David's storytelling."

— James in Pipe Creek, Texas

"Wow! You were in Hyder, Alaska before I put the book down the first time! Your narrative made me feel like I was almost there with you. I really appreciate the insights during the prep, the ride, and in hindsight. The best part is that you've made me excited about pursuing my own BIG DREAM. I would definitely recommend this book to anyone that has a dream or who enjoys riding. Thank you for sharing your adventure!"

— Lisa in Birmingham, Alabama

MOTORCYCLE DREAM RIDE

Also by David Mixson

Motorcycle Smarts: Overcome Fear, Learn Control, Master Riding Well

(Book 1 in the 'Motorcycle Smarts' Book Series)

Motorcycle Hacks: Everything My Motorcycle Mentors Taught Me
—and More

(Book 3 in the 'Motorcycle Smarts' Book Series)

Motorcycle Dream Ride

My Alabama to Alaska Adventure

David Mixson

Copyright and Disclaimers

Motorcycle Dream Ride: My Alabama to Alaska Adventure

Copyright © 2021 by David Mixson

motorcyclesmarts.com

All rights reserved. Except as permitted under the U.S. Copyright Act of 1976, no part of this publication may be reproduced, distributed, or transmitted in any form or by any means, or stored in a database or retrieval system, without the prior written permission of the publisher.

Book cover design by Farid Arifudin and Caitlin Leigh Skaalrud.

Disclaimer

While all attempts have been made to verify the information provided in this publication, neither the author nor the publisher assumes any responsibility for errors, omissions, or contrary interpretations of the subject matter herein. The views expressed are those of the author alone, and should not be taken as expert instruction or imperatives. The reader is responsible for his or her own actions. Version 020723.

Laws and Regulations

Adherence to all applicable traffic laws, rules of the road, and motorcycle regulations —including international, federal, state, and local laws—is the sole responsibility of the purchaser or reader.

ISBN 978-1-7324532-4-1 (ebook)

ISBN 978-1-7324532-5-8 (paperback)

ISBN 978-1-7324532-6-5 (hardcover)

To Mike

for being an incredible friend and the real star in this book.
Did we really do this? At least we have these pages to refresh
our memories when dementia sets in. I can't imagine riding a
motorcycle to Alaska with anyone else.

Twenty years from now you will be more disappointed by the things you didn't do than the ones you did do. So throw off the bowlines. Sail away from the safe harbor. Catch the trade winds in your sails. Explore. Dream. Discover.

— MARK TWAIN

Contents

Foreword

By Maddie Mixson Cook
The Author's Favorite Daughter

There have only been a handful of times in my life when my Dad said or did something that totally surprised me.

One of the first times I can remember was when I was eleven years old, and he came home with a bright red motorcycle. I stared in disbelief and excitement because I knew getting a motorcycle was something he had dreamed of doing. He loved riding.

It was like he was a kid all over again—living his dream.

Fast Forward Ten Years

Here I was again, just like that eleven-year-old little girl, staring in disbelief and excitement when my Dad told us he was going to ride his motorcycle to Alaska with Mike.

Did I mention their goal was to do it in less than a month?

I knew they were going to have to book it.

I asked my Dad for one thing before his trip.

I thought it would be special if he and Mike left together from our house so Mom, Drew, and I could cheer them on. He obliged. *Seeing them off was a special moment for all of us.*

Fast Forward Five Years

Here I am again, just like that eleven-year-old little girl, staring in disbelief and excitement yet again because my Dad has completed another big dream—to write this book.

I can hardly wait to read about his journey and learn the small details he may have left out when he told us about his trip.

Thank you, Dad, for showing me how to live your dreams, no matter how old you are or how long you have to wait. And thank you for showing me patience—because neither of your big dreams would have come true without it.

Overcoming Excuses

One year before departure …

One of my DREAMS is to ride a motorcycle somewhere far away. I want to disconnect from work and my daily life in a meaningful way. I want to experience something totally new. I want to ride so far from home that I feel uncomfortable.

But I'm good at rationalizing away my dreams, and I bet you are too. Mine goes something like this.

I have one child in college, and a second one is starting soon.

I don't have the money to ride somewhere for no purpose.

I have a job, and my boss won't like me taking off.

I have a family who depends on me.

My body might not hold up to that much riding.

I can live my dreams later.

But these are nothing but lame excuses. There are no guarantees. In the last two weeks, a friend was diagnosed with cancer, and a work colleague dropped dead after a massive heart attack.

I can't afford excuses—and neither can you.

Just Four Things

Through this journey of self-discovery, I've come to the conclusion that I only need four things to turn any DREAM into a reality.

1. money
2. time away from work and home
3. reasonably good health
4. a desire and skill to do it

Mike and I have everything we need. Money isn't a huge issue. We're both in pretty good health—no back pain, prostate issues, knee pain, or incontinence problems (geez, we're not that old).

Time away from my normal life isn't a major problem either. My kids are old enough to manage themselves, and I'm not as critical at work as I'd like to pretend.

So ...

What do *you* dream about doing but haven't?

What excuses are getting in *your* way?

Introduction

This book isn't just for motorcyclists. It's for anyone who DREAMS of doing something magical but gets stuck in EXCUSES and SELF-DOUBTS. It's for anyone who needs encouragement to do that SOMETHING they've always wanted to do but haven't.

When I was twelve, I begged my parents for a motorcycle. They said no, so I settled for an orange Honda Express moped.

Nearly three decades later, I decided for myself that I wanted a motorcycle and bought one. Then ten years after that (at fifty), I ventured outside my comfort zone and set out to ride from Huntsville, Alabama to Hyder, Alaska (and back) with my best friend.

I wrote this book so Mike and I can remember what we experienced along the way—the people we met and the challenges we overcame. But bigger than that, I wrote this book to challenge you to LIVE YOUR BIG DREAM.

Our journey was less about making it to Alaska—and more about discovering things about ourselves we didn't know.

It was about uncovering goodness that often goes unnoticed.

It was about doing what we weren't sure was possible.

It was about overcoming FEAR.

I wrote ride reports at the end of each day and posted them online for friends and family to read. But I only told part of the story. This book peels back a layer and describes what was really going through my head before, during, and after our ride.

It also introduces the wonderful people we met along the way (something I didn't have time to fully develop in my daily reports) and describes some of the close calls I purposefully left out because our wives were following along.

Motorcycle Dream Ride is the second book in the *Motorcycle Smarts* book series. This book is broken into three main sections:

PART ONE takes you behind the scenes and shows you how we prepared for the trip, why we selected Alaska, and how our family and friends reacted when we told them we wanted to take time away from our normal lives to ride somewhere far away.

PART TWO gives a moment-by-moment account of the ride. In this section, I also added chapters between ride reports (many set in a different time) to give the backstory of our journey.

And finally, in the APPENDIX I give a personal challenge, share trip statistics (miles, cost, ride time), and Mike and I answer your frequently asked questions.

Throughout the book, I've added my thoughts from a perspective of one year later. I call these sections *Reflections One Year Later.* This is where I share some of the untold stories and describe how the events of the day affected me.

With a little prodding, Mike added his perspective in several spots, which I believe adds depth and balance.

Hold on Tight

Instead of going in exact chronological order, I jump around a bit. When I do this, I'll let you know at the beginning of the chapter by writing something like, "Two weeks before departure."

It's also probably worth mentioning that I sometimes refer to a *motorcycle* as a *bike*. I started doing this because Mike does it. My parents were right. You are influenced by the friends you hang out with. And finally, I refer to our motorcycles, the BMW R1200GS, as a "GS" for short.

Getting It Right

This book makes me nervous. Only two people know what really happened on this adventure. Mike, I hope I presented it in a way that honors our friendship and accurately documents our journey.

If I missed this mark, I've failed miserably.

Part how-to, part documentary, part personal discovery—this is a story about two friends doing something they'd made excuses not to do for years. It's a story about exploration, perseverance—and friendship. It's a story about SILENCING the I CAN'T DO THAT inner voice that lives in all of us.

Part One: Preparing for the Ride

This section takes you behind the scenes of our trip and describes what happened before we departed, why we chose Alaska, how we got approval from home and work, and why we selected our bikes. *It also reveals some of the struggles we encountered in the process.*

ONE

Planning Phase

Fourteen months before departure ...

Mike and I were eating lunch when he announced.
"I'm going to ride my motorcycle to Alaska."
I paused for a moment to see if he was joking.
He wasn't.
"Are you crazy?"
"We *should* be able to ride to Alaska and back in four weeks."
Like a brainwashed cubicle slave, I instinctively responded.
"I can't take that much time off work."
Then I changed the subject.

After some serious self-reflection and debate with myself over the next several days, I concluded that Mike's crazy idea wasn't so crazy and that the only things keeping us from riding to Alaska were my excuses.

Several days later, I gave him the news.
"Mike, I think we should do it."

The Route

Mike took the lead planning the route. At one point, he suggested that we might want to pick somewhere closer. "It's a long way to Alaska. I'm not sure we can ride that far in the time we have."

In a text, Mike suggested Nova Scotia as an option.

"Where the hell is Nova Scotia?" I replied.

After several attempts, I managed to get the destination spelled correctly in Google. While Nova Scotia looked like a great place to ride, I preferred the twelve-syllable simplicity of saying:

"I'm riding my motorcycle to Alaska."

I figured if we were going big, we should stick to the original plan—and GO BIG.

Mike agreed. Alaska it was.

Getting Approval

Once Mike and I decided on a destination, I sought approval from two women—my wife, Sue, and my boss, Jeri.

I knew Sue wouldn't like the idea. She's always wanted to travel out West, and when I tell her I want to ride my bike there without her, on the way to Alaska, another spot she's always wanted to see, she's really going to be jealous.

Have I mentioned she has red hair? Just so you know, it *might* be true what they say about redheads having a temper.

I decided to introduce the idea one night at dinner.

"Mike and I are thinking about riding to Alaska."

After a few awkward moments of silence and a look like she'd taken a mouthful of sour milk, she said exactly one word.

"Why?"

I tried to explain, but I knew she wouldn't understand.

She doesn't ride a motorcycle and has no desire to. Knowing this, my words sounded futile, even to me. She took a deep breath. "I want to take my dream vacation to Europe."

Neither of her responses surprised me. I had already figured if my trip to Alaska cost me X dollars, then something she wanted would cost me twice that. That's the mental calculation I always make when I do fun stuff without her.

Several days later, she informed me that she wanted to take the family vacation to Europe *before* my motorcycle trip. In her words, "Just in case you crash and break a leg."

"Honey, if I crash, my injuries will almost certainly be worse." I should have remained silent.

Asking my boss at work was easier. "Jeri, I'm thinking about taking off a month next summer to ride my motorcycle to Alaska."

Her face lit up. "Oh my gosh. That sounds so exciting!"

Reflections One Year Later

I didn't tell many of my friends I was riding to Alaska, and I'm not sure why. Maybe it's because I wasn't positive I could make it and didn't want to be embarrassed. Or maybe it's because I don't like being the center of attention, or because it sounded boastful, or that I'm more impressed with what someone *has* done rather than what they say they're *going* to do.

Our 24-day window to make it to Alaska and back wasn't as long as we had wished for. As you'll soon find out, unfortunately, this window would have to be shortened even more.

TWO

Final Details

Four months before departure …

I t's four months before we're scheduled to leave.

Mike has planned the route, scouted for hotels and campsites along the way, and scheduled contingency options.

For this, I am grateful.

I'm the navigator in my family and welcome the break. I know
I'll enjoy the adventure more if I don't have to be glued to a map.

Mike asked for inputs, and I gave him three:

(1) I prefer to stay in a hotel on really long ride days.

*(2) I prefer to have short days and long days—instead of having
all ride days the same distance.*

(3) I prefer the route to and from Alaska to be different.

I think he was surprised at my limited inputs. But I know the
route he plans will be better than the one I imagine, and I don't
want to screw that up by giving him too many suggestions.

The Plan

The most direct route to Alaska has us crossing into Canada from Minnesota, but we both want to attend the BMW Motorcycle Owners of America rally in Billings, Montana on the way.

So the current plan is to ride to Billings for the rally, and from there to head north, cross into Canada, and then ride northwest to Hyder. I figure Mike has a few detours planned for the trip, and I'm fairly certain he's Googled *top ten motorcycle roads* more than a time or two.

At least, I hope he has.

Our lives are giving us a window of 24 days to make it there and back. Not as many as we would like, but we'll claim them.

I've decided not to bring a GPS. There's no need to have two cooks in the kitchen. Mike has a Garmin, and he knows how to use it. In a pinch, I can use the GPS on my phone.

Perfect. That's one less thing I have to carry.

THREE

Selecting Bikes

Months before departure …

M ike has a fleet of motorcycles. I have one.
I've stopped trying to keep up with the exact number of bikes he has. I'm not positive he even knows.

Just between us, Mike keeps a handful of them at his mom's house in her storage shed. I wonder if his wife, Michelle knows.

He insists she does, but that she's just a wonderful person.

We went back and forth about what motorcycle we should ride on our adventure. Mike was more than happy for any excuse to add to his fleet. I was more interested in the practicality of riding the same bike: same fuel range, same riding position, and frankly, better photos. I think pictures look awesome when riders have the same bike. There, I said it. Good photos matter to me.

We decided on the BMW R1200 GS Adventure.

The Purchases

Mike's budget was bigger than mine. He started looking for a gently used GS, and I started looking for one with character.

In no time, Mike found a black GS located in a small town just outside Dallas, Texas. Three weeks later, Mike flew to Dallas, made the exchange, and rode it back to Alabama.

It took me a little longer, but I found a metallic-colored GS in Knoxville that fit my criteria. I borrowed Mike's motorcycle trailer (now you know why we're friends) to pick it up.

It was sitting in the driveway when I pulled up.

I asked the owner if he would ride it down the street so I could make sure it ran and shifted correctly. It did. I counted out a stack of hundred-dollar bills. He signed the title. And I headed home—thankful I had a bike to match Mike's.

Reflections One Year Later

On my drive back, I heard on the radio that someone had shot and killed five servicemen at a U.S. Navy Reserve center in Chattanooga, Tennessee. I stopped at Sugars BBQ for lunch, and CNN was carrying it live. I asked the hostess if the shooting was nearby.

"It's about a mile down the road."

I felt sick. Innocent people were shot and killed for no reason, and I was picking up a motorcycle for a joy ride to Alaska.

The drive back gave me time to think. I was torn.

When I pulled into my driveway, I felt relieved to have my biggest purchase behind me.

I felt blessed to have my family there safe inside.

FOUR

Practice Ride From Hell

Two days before departure ...

Mike and I just went for a ride to test our new headsets. Two miles out, it started raining. I told Mike inside my helmet that I needed to stop to secure my phone.

"Good thing the pocket on your new jacket is waterproof."

"That's neat," I said. "I didn't know that."

I pulled over and moved my phone from my pants pocket to the front pocket on my new Olympia riding jacket.

Then we continued.

We monkeyed with the headsets and figured out how to do the basics: connect the intercoms and call using our phones.

It felt odd talking to someone besides myself inside my helmet.

We pulled onto I-565 heading east, and it started pouring rain. Five miles later, I told Mike I was going to turn around at the next exit and head back home.

I could hardly see cars in front of me.

Mike lives in the opposite direction and said he was going to find a place to wait it out.

I took the next off-ramp, circled around, and reentered I-565, this time heading west toward home.

The rain was relentless.

The wind was blowing me around like a toy.

But I kept calm, confident my phone was secure and thankful I had worn my new BMW waterproof riding boots.

Home

When I turned into my neighborhood, the rain stopped. I pulled into my garage, took off my gloves and helmet, then unzipped the waterproof pocket in the front of my new riding jacket.

When I did, my phone was fully submerged in a pocket-full of water. It turns out the jacket pocket didn't keep water out, but it did a great job of keeping the water in.

Once I caught my breath, I realized that my feet were cold. I unzipped my left boot, and my sock was soaked. I turned the boot over, and water poured out.

I'm about to ride to Alaska, and my gear just failed me.

I knew I had to make adjustments.

I spread out my wet gear in my garage and hooked up a fan to dry it out. The last thing I want to do is ride to Alaska with soured gear. I visited the Verizon store that evening and signed a contract in exchange for a new phone.

I'm thankful for the lesson.

Reflections One Year Later

As it turns out, this test ride was a blessing. I upgraded my phone (better camera) and learned that I should never assume anything is waterproof. I also learned a valuable lesson. The most effective rain gear I can afford is the kind you put over your normal gear.

Before this ride, I wasn't planning on carrying my external rain jacket and pants, figuring the rain liner on my jacket would do.

After this ride, I decided to pack both.

A wise decision, as you'll soon find out.

FIVE

Title Problems
_____

Days before departure …

There's a problem with the title on Mike's bike that I've put
off mentioning until now.

When Mike tried to transfer ownership into his name, the lady
at the Alabama DMV said the title wasn't signed correctly and that
it would have to be fixed. The title was signed by Jared, the person
Mike bought it from, but it also needed to be signed by his wife
because she was listed on the title.

Mike texted Jared.

"I need your wife to sign a form from the DMV because she's
listed on the title."

"Well, that might be a problem," Jarad responded. "She's now
my ex-wife, and we went through a bitter divorce."

The plan was for Mike to send the form to Jared. Jared would
send it to his attorney. His attorney would send it to his ex-wife's
attorney. And his ex-wife's attorney would then send it to the ex-
wife for her to sign. Somewhere in this process (shockingly?), it
always lost momentum and never made it all the way through.

Everyone blamed each other, but in the meantime, Mike had paid money for a motorcycle he couldn't own.

When all this started, Mike was calm. "It's an honest mistake," he said. But two months later, with a trip to Alaska at risk, his patience was exhausted. He'd been promised that she was going to sign the title "tomorrow" for months. Mike was frustrated.

A Different Approach

Since it was just days before our departure and Mike still didn't have her signature, I suggested a different approach.

"Mike, she's dragging her feet because she thinks it's hurting her ex-husband. You should do something bold to get her attention. Why don't you bypass all the attorneys, contact her directly, and tell her she's destroying our dream ride to Alaska."

Mike knew her name and that she was a dentist in a small town outside Dallas. An hour later, Mike texted me that he'd sent her flowers. On the card, he had the florist write:

"Thank you for helping me get the title straightened out on the motorcycle. Mike [phone number]."

That afternoon she called Mike, thanked him for the flowers, and said she would sign (and have notarized) whatever he sent to her. We were both excited. At least Mike was in direct contact with the person who could make this happen, and she was willing to do the right thing.

Mike received the signed paperwork the next day. Unfortunately, her signature didn't match the name on the title exactly, so it had to be redone. Mike was really flustered now.

He emailed her and explained the error.

She replied, "I will redo it when I can."

Neither of us knew what to think about her response. Did this mean she would fix it today … or next week? We were scheduled to leave on Monday. Both bikes were packed and ready to go, but we were stuck in Alabama on standby.

Monday morning came—*nothing.*

Tuesday—*nothing.*

Let's Go

On Wednesday morning at 9:43 a.m. Mike texted:

"Received FedEx package. Headed to DMV."

I crossed my fingers, took a deep breath, and waited to hear. Thirty minutes later, Mike texted:

"Got tag. I'll be ready to pull out by noon."

My heart raced. I was excited. I was nervous.

Part Two: The Ride

This section brings you along with us as we set out to ride from Alabama to Alaska and back. I wrote a summary at the end of each day (in my tent, hotel room, or lobby) and posted it online. Here, I've added more details about what *really* happened (and how those events affected us) and shared new insights from the perspective of one year later. I've also sprinkled in other chapters along the way (set in a different time) that help complete our story.

I hope you'll be able to sense how the miles changed me.

First Leg

Huntsville, Alabama to Billings, Montana

The main focus on this leg of our journey was to travel from Alabama to Montana as quickly as possible so we could attend the BMW Motorcycle Owners of America (MOA) rally.

We spent most of each day riding on interstates.
It felt rushed and methodical—but good.

Alabama, Tennessee, Kentucky, Illinois, Missouri, Iowa, Nebraska, South Dakota, Wyoming, and Montana

SIX

Finding Myself

FLASHBACK: *Two weeks before departure …*

I n the past month, I've watched *City Slickers* and *Wild Hogs*—two movies centered around middle-aged men taking trips to find themselves.

While there are certainly points in both movies I can relate to, I'm not looking to find myself on the way to Alaska.

I accept that I've lost momentum at my job and that I could never become the President of the United States. Making it to the Olympics as a competitor is also off the table, just like completing a marathon in under four hours.

But there's a level of peace that comes with age.

I accept that I'll never have more kids, that I'll never become filthy rich, and that I'll most likely never get another big promotion at work. But I look at all this as a good thing.

I can be myself at work and admit my passions lie elsewhere.

I can choose my friends honestly and without calculation.

I can say "No Thanks!" when management holds out a carrot that requires sixty hours a week to snatch.

I can take off for a month and ride my motorcycle to Alaska without fear of retaliation.

I'm fifty now, and I can be me—finally.

I don't expect to find myself on this adventure ... mostly
BECAUSE I ALREADY HAVE.

SEVEN

Ride Day One

FINALLY

WEDNESDAY
HUNTSVILLE, ALABAMA TO MT. VERNON, ILLINOIS

After Mike's text that he had a legal title, I told Sue we were cleared to go.

She made eye contact with me but didn't say a word. It was as if she was surprised this moment was here. I think I was too.

A few minutes later, Mike sent a text that he'd be at my house in 30 minutes. I pulled the GS out of my garage, tugged on the dry bag strapped behind my seat one last time, and walked around my bike like a pilot walks around his airplane.

I hope I'm not forgetting something.

Right on time, Mike pulled up, and I started putting on my riding jacket. I knew we had a long way to go before dark. I kissed Sue goodbye one last time, hugged Maddie and Drew, and asked Mike if he was ready to ride. I reached for my helmet.

"Once I put this on, I'm leaving."

Mike rolled his eyes and said something about me getting grumpy when I'm hot. He knows me pretty well.

Our Departure

Mike and I rolled out of my driveway at 12:17 p.m. It was more than hot. Unfortunately, the best time to ride to Alaska without snow is during the middle of summer.

Guess I'll have to get over my phobia of riding in the heat.

Today was about one thing, making it to Mt. Vernon, Illinois (300 miles from home) via the fastest route possible.

From Huntsville, we headed north on Highway 53, then right onto I-65 heading north toward Nashville, Tennessee.

Everything felt good.

A few minutes later, Mike looked at the radar on his GPS.

"Dave, it looks like we're about to run into rain."

We learned something from our practice ride from hell, so we pulled over and put our phones in plastic bags.

Stopping on the side of an interstate was just as nerve-racking as I had imagined. With 18-wheelers whizzing past, we moved as quickly as possible. We were less than 60 miles into our journey, and we'd already broken one of our two rules—not to stop on the side of an interstate.

I hope this isn't a sign, I thought.

Once we were back underway, Mike told me he'd heard on the news that a truck driver on I-85 in North Carolina had fallen asleep and mowed over five motorcyclists who had pulled over on the shoulder. I'm not sure I really wanted to know that.

In Nashville (120 miles from home) we exited onto I-24 and rode for 55 miles to the Kentucky state line, then for another 50 miles through the southwest corner of Kentucky and into Illinois.

At the Illinois state sign welcoming us, I called for a photo stop. We pulled over, and I hurriedly snapped a few shots without getting off my bike.

Mike's story made an impact on me.

Final Destination

Eighty-five miles later, we arrived at the Drury Inn in Mt. Vernon, Illinois with daylight left to spare.

The hotel is nice. We took advantage of the complimentary salad and pasta buffet for dinner. It was reasonably good and made it where we didn't have to get back on our bikes—a huge plus in my mind.

Final Thoughts

I'm inside our hotel room writing this ride report.

We rode on interstates the entire day, and nothing struck me as extra special. I was more focused on getting into the rhythm of clicking through miles.

I've ridden most of these roads before.

I'm relieved to have the first day behind us and pleased with how well my GS performed. The riding position is as comfortable as any motorcycle I've ridden. But I also know that we've barely scratched the surface on this journey.

States Traveled: Alabama, Tennessee, Kentucky, and Illinois
Miles Ridden: 336.6

Reflections One Year Later

DAVID'S THOUGHTS

My mind was racing with doubts when we pulled out.

This day happened so fast. I feared I wasn't ready—physically or emotionally. Silently, I felt anxious.

I had no idea if I could complete this journey, even though I'd dreamed of doing it for nearly a year. I broke my back helping a friend move a refrigerator years ago, and sitting in a chair with no back just about kills me.

Yet, I'm riding to Alaska on a seat with no back. Brilliant.

I felt added pressure because someone else was depending on me. I knew my body would need to hold up for the next 21 days. How would I tell Mike I couldn't go any farther? How would I explain that his trip of a lifetime had to end because I was a pansy?

I could picture the look of disappointment on his face.

Days before we left, I secretly hoped the title problem on his motorcycle wouldn't get worked out. Then, I wouldn't have to face this moment of doubt. I kept my feelings to myself as we pulled away—just like guys are supposed to.

Part of me didn't want to go—and part of me felt like a kid who was about to see Santa Claus for the first time.

Can a man laugh and tear up at the same time?

When we rolled out of town, I was excited yet terrified. More than anything, though, I prayed that I wouldn't someday regret my decision to make this journey.

MIKE'S THOUGHTS

I was excited we were finally leaving Huntsville.

Months of looking at Google Maps was finally paying off.

It was humid and hot—just like I like it.

Leaving was almost anti-climactic following the stress of my title problems. I knew the moment we pulled out that all my planning would have to be redone.

We had two and a half days to make it to Billings for the rally.

We paid for the full event but would only be there for a day.

My original plan was to camp the first night (sort of a camping shake-down night), but David vetoed the camping. The Drury Inn was a nice oasis in the heat of summer.

We made it just in time for dinner.

Day One was done, but I knew hard days were ahead.

David and Mike Ready to Head Out

Our First Rule Broken on I-65 South of Nashville

Hello Tennessee

Hello Kentucky

Hello Illinois

EIGHT

My Bike's Second Trip to Alaska

SOMEONE IMPORTANT OWNED HER FIRST

FLASHBACK: *Several days before departure …*

W hen I purchased my GS, the seller pulled out a copy of the original bill of sale that showed Franklin Graham, Billy Graham's son, as the original owner.

For a moment, I thought it might be a sign, but I don't think God has time for that sort of thing. Later that night, I told Sue.

"Guess who used to own the motorcycle I just bought."

"Who?" she asked."

"Billy Graham's son."

"Well, that's a good sign. Maybe you won't die on it."

Her response wasn't what I expected, but I kept quiet. Decades of marriage has taught me the value of silence. A few minutes later, I overheard her on the phone telling a friend.

I did some additional research and found a video of Franklin setting out for Alaska on his GS. It turns out my motorcycle has been to Alaska once already.

Great. At least one of us has done this before.

My father was a minister too, which means Franklin and I are both preacher's kids. If everything goes as planned, we'll have one more thing in common in a few weeks.

We will both have ridden the same motorcycle to Alaska.

NINE

Ride Day Two

THE GATEWAY ARCH

THURSDAY

MT. VERNON, ILLINOIS TO SIOUX CITY, IOWA

Today was our first morning on the road, and we fumbled around establishing a routine. Mike got up first and started getting ready, and I started packing since I showered last night.

When I took my stuff down and started loading my bike, the first thing I noticed was that all my gear didn't fit in my side cases as easily as it did yesterday.

By the time I made it to breakfast, Mike was already there. We ate mostly carbs, caught up on the national news, then Mike went back to the room to get his gear while I finished eating.

The buffet was good, and I enjoyed the vacation feel.

Today was about making it as far as we could in the direction of Billings, Montana. The BMW rally starts there on Saturday, and the delay in getting Mike's title caused us to play catch up.

We wanted to make it to Sioux City, Iowa (600 miles away) by sundown.

I had never ridden a motorcycle that far in one day.

We met up at the GSs a few minutes later. Mike, the navigator, punched a few buttons on his GPS and said, "You ready?"

He led the way out of the parking lot, and we turned right on I-57 heading north. A few miles later, we took I-64 heading west toward St. Louis, Missouri.

The Gateway Arch

Eighty miles later, signs signaled we were getting close to St. Louis. Nothing says welcome to the West like the Gateway Arch. It was a clear, blue day. We spotted the Arch well outside the city.

I'm amazed every time I see it.

As we continued west, the Arch got bigger—signaling we were heading in the right direction. A few miles outside of the city, we exited onto I-70 heading northwest and continued around to the north side of St. Louis.

"Mike, we should exit and get a photo by the Arch."

He wasn't super excited about my idea (probably because we had a long way to ride), but he could hear the passion in my voice.

He conceded.

"Since you've been there, why don't you lead the way."

I didn't have a GPS but figured it would be easy enough to find. We exited, and I took the lead heading southeast back toward the Arch. With traffic and one-way streets to battle, finding the Arch wasn't as easy as I had imagined, but we found it.

More on that in the next chapter.

We took several shots, then found I-70 again and pushed west.

BMWs and Fuel Tank Sensors

An hour and a half outside of St. Louis, I started running low on fuel. Since GSs are prone to having fuel tank sensor problems, I told Mike I wanted to ride a little farther so I could test my low fuel warning indicator.

"That's fine. Just let me know when you want to stop."

Just west of Danville, Missouri, my GS computer signaled a low fuel warning.

Perfect, I thought. It's working just like it should.

"Mike, I'm fine to stop at the next gas station."

"Okay, I'll start looking."

Meanwhile, 10 miles passed, then 20. No gas stations. About that time, my GS warned that I had seven miles of fuel left.

"Mike, I'm about to run out of gas!"

My good intentions turned into a pit in my stomach.

We took the next exit onto Highway 1005 in hopes of finding something—anything. At the end of the exit ramp, a sign showed gas to the left. We gently headed that way.

One mile later, we spotted an old abandoned gas station.

Doesn't anybody use gas around here? A handmade sign read, "Closest gas five miles" (with an arrow pointing north).

I didn't know if I could make it, but it was our best option.

It felt like we were in the middle of nowhere, but we trusted the sign was correct and continued.

Thankfully, we made it the five miles to Crane's Country Store in Williamsburg, Missouri without having to push.

I was thrilled.

The simple things in life are the easiest to take for granted.

Crane's Country Store

Crane's reminded me of a country store near my grandparents' house when I was a kid. I pulled up to one of the two pumps and immediately noticed there wasn't a credit card slot.

Here, patrons pump gas first, then pay inside.

It's been a long time since I've done that.

We both filled up, then went inside to pay and look around.

A group of nine men was sitting in a circle eating sandwiches, laughing, and having a grand time.

They called themselves the "Thursday Liars Club."

When we told them we were headed to Alaska, half of them thought we were crazy. The other half wanted to go with us.

We drank a Diet Sun Drop, paid for our gas, and wished we could have stayed longer. Instead, we suited up and continued on I-70 toward Kansas City, Missouri (160 miles away).

Kansas City BBQ

For lunch, Mike suggested we eat at Arthur Bryant's BBQ.

He knew I would like the idea.

In Kansas City, we exited and found our way there a few miles south off the interstate. A security guard greeted us and motioned for us to park inside the razor wire fence around back. I felt uneasy that he was there but relieved at the same time. I grabbed my laptop and helmet—and left everything else to fate.

Partway through the meal, I went to the restroom and was horrified to see the parking lot security guard walk in behind me. I thought about asking him who was watching our bikes in his absence but decided that would only delay him from getting back to work.

We finished eating, then anxiously walked to our motorcycles. Thankfully, everything was there, so we suited up in the Kansas City heat and continued.

We made our way back to I-70, then a few miles later, we exited onto I-29 heading north toward Sioux City, Iowa.

Our Neighbor

Our next stop was for gas and a Diet Mountain Dew (200 miles from lunch) at a truck stop just across the state line from Omaha, Nebraska. The break felt good.

When we returned to our bikes, a truck driver walked up and asked if we were from Huntsville, Alabama.

"Yes," we answered.

"I live in Guntersville," he said.

Guntersville is a small town about 30 miles east of Huntsville. It's also just a few miles away from where Mike grew up.

Bubba (I don't recall his real name) was hauling a load of dog food for Walmart. We had only been gone for one day, but I was happy to see a friendly face who knew our home. I told him we were keeping a photo journal of our trip and asked if he minded if I took a selfie of the three of us.

"No problem."

Then we said goodbye and suited up.

Our ride on I-29 kept us in Iowa, east of the Missouri River, but ever so close to the Nebraska line. I had never been there, so I suggested to Mike that we ride into Nebraska to get a photo of the state road sign.

He agreed.

When we exited the parking lot, we turned right and rode about five miles to the Nebraska state line, stopped for a photo, then made a u-turn and backtracked to the original route.

Stuff like this makes long days longer but more enjoyable.

Final Destination

Hours later, we pulled into the Holiday Inn in Sioux City, Iowa at sunset. I was thrilled to see a Chili's next to the hotel. This meant we could walk to dinner (no riding gear, no riding at night), and I could have a beer. I was happy. I was also thankful that the navigator planned this on purpose because he knew I'd like it.

Final Thoughts

It seems like we left a week ago, but it was only yesterday.

That's probably not a good sign.

Missouri and Iowa are beautiful—filled with corn and soybean fields for as far as the eye can see. I probably saw more corn today than I've seen (cumulatively) in my entire life. Corn looks greener here than in Alabama.

It was a hard day of riding, but compared to what?

I'd rather be here than at work—or most anywhere.

Who gets to say that?

States Traveled: Illinois, Missouri, Iowa, and Nebraska
Miles Ridden: 605.3

Reflections One Year Later

Six hundred miles is a long way to ride a motorcycle I had just purchased. My butt was killing me—already.

In addition to that, the speaker from the helmet headset was passionately pushing on the top of my left ear. I adjusted everything but never could make the pain go away.

I knew changing helmets right before the trip was risky.

Silence gave me plenty of time to think inside my helmet. Two days in, and I was already questioning whether I could make it.

I didn't share these doubts with Mike.

On a positive note, the riding position on the GS fit perfectly. My back, arms, and legs all felt great. Unfortunately, this gave my brain plenty of energy to focus on my ear and butt pain.

Nearly running out of gas taught us a valuable lesson. From that point forward, we filled up more often. But I'm thankful for the experience because Crane's Country store was one of the unexpected jewels on our trip. It's hard to explain the charm of the place and how comforting it was to see the "Thursday Liars Club."

Those men don't have Facebook followers. They have real friendships. WE SHOULD ALL BE JEALOUS.

Crane's is the way it used to be and the way I want it to be again. I would have enjoyed pulling up a chair and hearing their stories.

I think we would have stayed and talked if this had happened later on our trip. It took us a while to realize that meeting people along the way would be one of the best parts.

Arthur Bryant's was a huge disappointment. Average food with horrible service made the experience a bust for me. I felt like the staff was put out that we were there.

When I spilled my tea, our waitress looked at me as if to say: "I ain't helping you clean that up." And she didn't.

If this is the best of Kansas City style BBQ, no thanks.

Thursday Liars Club

Bubba from Guntersville

Hello Missouri

Hello Iowa

Hello Nebraska

TEN

Our First Argument

O ur first falling-out was in St. Louis after I insisted we take a photo at the Gateway Arch.

I took the lead when we exited downtown. I didn't have a GPS but figured it would be easy enough to spot.

I should have known better.

I found the Arch, but I lost Mike in the process.

One moment he was right behind me, and the next, he wasn't. The headsets worked great when we were close to each other, but not so great when we were around tall buildings.

We were around tall buildings.

"Mike, can you hear me? Mike. Mike, can you hear me?"

Nothing.

When I lost him, I couldn't help but fear that he had crashed. He was just behind me, and I hadn't made any quick lane changes. I found a place to pull over and kept trying.

He didn't respond.

This is the exact thing helmet headsets are made for, but ours didn't work. I was frustrated and worried. We hadn't even made it through Illinois, and Mike has crashed.

I tried calling Mike using the phone feature without success. I'm not sure if it was user error or headset error. It has a bunch of buttons, and I wasn't as good at using them this early in the trip.

Maybe the headset didn't understand cuss words.

Minutes later, Mike rode up, and our headsets reconnected.

Now that I knew he was okay, I got mad. I felt like a worried parent who had found his lost child.

"What happened?" I asked.

"I got caught at the light."

I didn't recall running through a yellow and couldn't understand why he had fallen behind. I wasn't happy.

"Is there a reason you can't keep up with me?" Silence.

We found the Arch, pulled over and took several selfies faking smiles, then left St. Louis in silence. Once we found the interstate, we didn't talk for the next hour.

By lunch, we were over it.

Faking Smiles at the Gateway Arch

ELEVEN

Ride Day Three

THE LONGEST DAY

FRIDAY
SIOUX CITY, IOWA TO BILLINGS, MONTANA

The BMW rally in Billings, Montana starts tomorrow, and today was about making it there.

From the moment we got up, I could sense from Mike's body language that today was different. I knew Billings was a long way away, but I didn't know exactly how long.

I told Mike I wanted to keep it that way.

We packed with a sense of urgency (mostly without talking), slammed down a CLIF Bar, and rolled out at 7:30 a.m.

My GS said it was 77 degrees.

Mike's said it was 78.

United Flight 232

As we pulled out, I wondered where the Sioux City airport was—the scene of a DC-10 crash in 1989 that I've read so much about.

The rear engine on United Flight 232 en route from Denver to

Chicago exploded and ruptured the primary and backup hydraulic systems. Without hydraulics, the pilots couldn't move the control surfaces to guide the aircraft.

United Airlines flight instructor Denny Fitch was onboard as a passenger and offered his assistance.

Captain Alfred Haynes accepted.

Fitch rushed to the flight deck and quickly devised a system of turning the aircraft by increasing and decreasing the throttles on the two remaining engines.

The pilots did an incredible job but crashed at the Sioux City airport, killing 112 of the 296 passengers on board.

I met Denny in 2011 at a NASA conference.

Denny was a magnetic speaker. I had heard him talk about the crash numerous times but never in person until then.

I was deeply moved every time I heard him speak. Twenty-plus years after the crash, Denny still got choked up when he described to us what happened on Flight 232.

Denny autographed a brochure for me. I still have it.

In 2012, Denny passed away after a battle with brain cancer.

I enjoy studying airplane crashes. At several points throughout my career, I've wondered how it might have been to work for the NTSB investigating airplane crashes instead of working at NASA.

Back to Our Adventure

From our hotel, we turned onto I-29 heading north, and crossed into South Dakota a few miles later. Eighty miles down the road, we exited onto I-90 heading west in Sioux Falls, South Dakota.

It was a beautiful day.

I knew we were stuck on I-90 for the foreseeable future, so I had no choice but to break one of our rules (again) and call for a photo stop to capture the moment.

We pulled to the side, took a few photos, and continued.

A few miles later, I called out to Mike in my helmet.

"How far out of the way is Mount Rushmore?"

"David, we have a long way to go today."

"Is it hours out of our way, or more like 20 minutes?"

No answer.

Silence told me my second guess was closer. I dropped it for now, but I wasn't done.

Marriage has taught me that timing is everything.

We still had a long way to go before this ride day was over, so we kept the throttle rolled back a little more than normal as we continued on I-90 for what felt like an eternity.

Corn and More Corn

Iowa and South Dakota were spectacular. Cornfields bordered soybean fields and more cornfields. It was mostly flat, and I could see corn for forever—in all directions.

Now I know where ethanol comes from.

I couldn't help but compare the landscape to home. The interstate median and shoulder are flatter and narrower than I'm used to, and it looks like they cut and bail the grass on it.

Why don't we do this in Alabama? Sounds like a good idea.

I noticed something else unusual—no trees. At points during our ride, I had to look hard to see anything sticking out of the ground more than a few feet that wasn't man-made.

Ride I-65 through Alabama, and you'll see trees the entire way.

When we crossed over the Missouri River near Chamberlain, South Dakota, everything changed—like I had awoken in another place.

Flat was replaced with rolling hills and rock formations. Cornfields were replaced with deep green fields of grass.

This didn't last, and the cornfields returned. But the contrast made me appreciate what I'd seen a few miles back.

Wall Drug

As we continued west, signs started appearing along the interstate advertising a place called Wall Drug. After about the fifth sign, Mike asked me if I was familiar with it.

"No, but if you want to stop, that's fine with me."

I could tell he wanted to stop and knew this was my hook for swinging by Mount Rushmore.

He took the bait.

By now, we had been on I-90 for almost 300 miles, and both of us were ready for a break. We exited in Wall, South Dakota, and found Wall Drug a few miles north of the interstate.

Everyone traveling on I-90 must have seen the same signs. The place was packed, and it took us several minutes to find a single parking spot to share.

Wall Drug is like Harrods in London, but not as fancy. Mike seemed to really enjoy exploring the zillion-square-foot facility. We shopped, ate lunch, then headed back to our bikes and suited up.

We turned south out of the parking lot and caught back up with I-90 (our home for most of the day) a few miles later.

Once we had clicked through some miles, I asked again.

"So, how far out of the way do you *really* think Mount Rushmore is?" Mike knew I was going to ask again and was ready.

"It looks like it's about 20 miles off the interstate."

"I want to go," I said.

"Okay, then we need to take Exit 61 heading south."

Mount Rushmore

We rode for another 50 miles, had a miscommunication issue that involved raising our voices, then regrouped at Exit 61. The headsets are 90 percent joy and 10 percent pure frustration.

Electronics are sometimes like that.

So is marriage. Several months ago, I told Sue that I wanted to write a book called "Living with Three Redheads," where I try to explain what it's like living in a house with three redheads—one wife, two children.

For some reason, she didn't like the idea—shocking?

From I-90 we took Highway 16 heading south. Thirty minutes later, we arrived at Mount Rushmore National Memorial.

It's free to get into the Memorial but costs $11 to park.

Mike was bummed about having to pay for two parking passes since together we take a single spot.

He voiced his concerns to the lady taking money.

She gave him a look from hell, so he dropped it.

By the time we parked, my hydration pack (yes, we wore water packs over our riding jackets) had been dry for hours. I needed water before I could fully appreciate the beauty around me. I told Mike I needed to find water and that we could meet up near the big rock. Surely, we couldn't screw that up.

I spotted a nice filtered water station and loitered around it until I'd consumed four tall glasses of water. I wondered if people noticed. I'm betting I looked pretty pitiful.

I filled my hydration pack with water and headed outside. It felt good to think clearly again. Water is a wonderful thing.

Minutes later, I found Mike on the path to the presidents.

We toured the museum and watched a History Channel film that explained everything about the place. Mike purchased several patches at the gift shop. Then we headed back to our bikes.

The excursion took longer than it should have, but I enjoyed every minute. The park is well-designed and easy to experience.

We suited up and headed back in the direction we had come. The ride down the mountain was almost as spectacular as the park. The afternoon sun was glowing on the valley below, just right.

Sturgis

Once we turned back onto I-90, we were about 40 miles from Sturgis, South Dakota. As it turns out, official Sturgis is next week.

Thousands of riders were getting a head start, and cruiser-type bikes dominated the interstate. I wanted to exit and ride through town but resisted the temptation to suggest it.

I had just used my silver bullet for the day.

A little past Sturgis, Mike's GPS suggested we take Highway 212 instead of following I-90 down and around to Montana.

We followed her advice.

A few miles after we exited, we clipped the northeast corner of Wyoming before crossing into Montana. We pulled over at both state signs to document our progress. Both stops were enjoyable—mostly because we weren't on an interstate.

Highway 212 took us through the Northern Cheyenne Indian Reservation and revealed parts of South Dakota, Wyoming, and Montana that we wouldn't have seen on I-90.

For nearly 100 miles, we saw nothing but nature—no houses, no barns, no buildings.

In a way, the experience felt odd.

In another, it felt incredibly peaceful.

Thankfully, we had just filled our nine-gallon GS fuel tanks and were averaging over 40 miles per gallon.

Then There Was Darkness

We rode into the most magnificent sunset—good enough to be in the closing credits of a Tom Hanks movie. We pulled over to freeze the moment, but a picture can only capture so much.

We were a long way from Billings and breaking our second rule—not to ride at night. But since we wanted to make it to the BMW rally, this was our only option.

Road signs signaled we were getting closer, but not quickly enough. We were exhausted and talked less and less. I suppose this was our price to pay for Wall Drug and Mount Rushmore.

Once it was dark, we worried about wild critters darting in front of us, so we let cars pass in the hope they would scare off anything in our path. I guess it worked.

We were both struggling.

It was hard for me to form a mental picture of what it looked like when we pulled out of our hotel parking lot this morning. To break the silence, I asked Mike if he wanted to sing, but he didn't hear me, or maybe he chose to ignore me, or maybe I thought I spoke those words out loud but didn't.

Out in the distance, we saw a spectacular lightning storm. I longed to pull over and take a photo but knew not to suggest it. We didn't need to extend this night any longer than it already was.

A few miles later, Mike pulled up his weather radar.

"Dave, it looks like we're about to ride into rain."

By this point, I felt numb and emotionless.

We looked for a gas station close to I-90. But the only thing we could find was an abandoned Citgo gone out of business. This seems to be a common theme for us on this trip.

The place felt creepy in the dark, but we stopped anyway.

We put on our rain gear, then took I-90 heading north.

Minutes later, Mike's GS flashed a low fuel warning message.

We took the next exit. Two engineers don't usually make the same mistake twice—unless it involves a woman.

Gas Stop

We exited in Hardin, Montana and found an Exxon. Let's just say Hardin at 11 p.m. on a Friday night isn't a place I care to revisit.

We filled up and proceeded inside to use the restroom.

We should have just held it.

Once inside, a man who looked crazy or on drugs walked by and gave me an uncomfortable glare. Seconds later, a sheriff ran in and confronted the man about shoplifting.

The sheriff then asked him to leave.

The man was upset. I didn't know how this was going to end, but I knew I didn't want to stick around to find out.

When I walked out, the man started following me. I mounted my bike as fast as I could, trying not to look like I was in a hurry.

The man continued toward me in a daze—just like they do on *The Walking Dead* but without his arms extended. I put on my helmet as fast as I could—I liked the advantage of head armor— and tossed my gloves onto the GS gauges to save time. And as fast as I could, I cranked my bike and moved to another spot.

I kept her running, just in case.

Sure, I could have waited for Mike to finish suiting up before pulling away, but someone needed to be ready to dial 9-1-1, right? Besides, Mike was at a pump two rows over, which gave him some extra time to finish before the crazy man got to him.

We pulled out of the parking lot a little wiser and a little more exhausted. As we rode off, I couldn't help but think of what my Dad used to tell me.

"Son, nothing good happens after 10 p.m."

He was right.

By now, it was 11:15 p.m. and we were 30 miles from Billings. Every mile was a struggle. It started raining, but not too hard. We rode at a slower pace than normal because we knew we were not at our best. The simple mechanics of riding took focus.

Maybe we shouldn't have made all those detours.

Final Destination

Mike navigated us without incident to our hotel for the evening. For that, I am thankful.

The hotel parking lot is packed with BMW motorcycles.

It's a beautiful sight but hard to appreciate at the moment.

We found a small unclaimed parking spot, took a handful of photos to document our condition, and checked in. Since we are staying two nights, I unloaded most of my gear (way too much).

What a day!

States Traveled: Iowa, South Dakota, Wyoming, and Montana
Miles Ridden: 803.2

Reflections One Year Later

Before we left for the day, we took a photo holding up three fingers, signifying it was Ride Day Three.

Too bad it took me two days to come up with that idea.

This was our longest ride day of the trip, but I'm glad we did it. Yes, we made mistakes. But one year later, I remember the positive aspects of the day more vividly: Wall Drug was interesting, Mount Rushmore was worth every minute, and the beautiful landscapes around us were breathtaking.

Looking back, this day was a good thing because it made our other long days seem shorter. It turns out, one of the best ways to make a 500-mile day seem easy is to ride 800 miles in a day.

Sounds silly, but it turned out to be a powerful tool.

When we parked on the top level of the concrete parking deck at Mount Rushmore, I thought I was about to explode. It was the hottest moment on the trip for me and the second hottest I've ever been in my life.

It must have been the combination of the parking deck around us radiating heat, waiting in line with no air circulation when we pulled up to park, and the fact that my water pack had been dry for hours. I wasn't just a little thirsty.

I couldn't think of anything else but water.

I also learned something about Mike. When he stops to see something, he likes to consume it all. At Wall Drug, he wanted to investigate every section. At Mount Rushmore, he didn't want to leave until he'd consumed every plaque and video.

No quickie stops for Mike.

And it only took me 25 years to figure that out.

I'm pretty quick.

My original description in the ride report of the gas station incident was toned down so Sue and Michelle wouldn't worry. I added more details above. When the man followed me to my bike, I thought something bad was about to happen.

This was a pivotal day on our adventure. I figured if we could survive this day (physically and emotionally), we could probably handle the next, and the next.

I think traveling is about give-and-take. I did things that Mike wanted to do, and he did things I wanted to do. The balance kept things working smoothly. He didn't care about Mount Rushmore, and I didn't care about Wall Drug.

We stopped at both—and we're better friends for it.

Corn and More Corn

Mount Rushmore

Staying Hydrated in the Heat

Amazing Sunset

Hello South Dakota

Hello Wyoming

Hello Montana

Beginning of Ride Day Three

End of Ride Day Three

TWELVE

Dad – Are You Nervous?

FLASHBACK: *One day before departure ...*

At dinner tonight, my son, Drew, asked.
"*Dad, are you nervous?*"
Without hesitation, I said "yes."
He looked surprised.
The truth is, I am apprehensive about the trip.
I've never ridden a motorcycle across the United States. I hate riding in the heat, and I wonder if I can even make it.
Thoughts of "what if" race through my mind.
What do we do if one of us gets sick, or crashes, or something bad happens back home?
Will they turn me away at the border because I don't have the correct paperwork or because another David Mixson committed a horrible crime once?
Did the guy sell my bike because it breaks down all the time?
How will my body handle the trip?
Will Mike and I get along?
Will my new helmet push my cheeks into my brain?

Will wearing a helmet for this long cause my hair to fall out?
Will Mike think I'm insane when he hears me talk to myself?
Will my riding gear keep me cool enough, warm enough?
Will thugs steal stuff off our bikes when we stop to eat?
Will our credit cards work in Canada?
Will we have phone coverage?
Will we encounter a hungry bear?
Will my side cases leak?
Will my laptop survive the trip?
What if my tires wear out?
Are mosquitos really that bad in Alaska?

YES—DADS GET NERVOUS TOO ... EVEN THOUGH WE DON'T LIKE TO ADMIT IT.

THIRTEEN

Ride Day Four

BMW MOTORCYCLE RALLY

SATURDAY
BILLINGS, MONTANA

Today we stayed in Billings all day and attended the BMW
Motorcycle Owners of America rally. Mike selected a hotel
within walking distance so we wouldn't have to get on our bikes.

My backside appreciates the break.

Even though we arrived late last night, we woke up early this
morning so we could register in time to hear the first lecture on
Controlling Your Motorcycle.

We made it to the session a few minutes before 8 a.m., and the
room was packed. I had no idea BMW owners were so studious.

If you ignored the guy who kept asking dumb questions and
sharing anecdotes about *his* riding experiences, the discussion was
informative. Why is it that there's always one person in every audi-
ence who asks stupid questions and derails the speaker?

Annoying.

BMW Rallies

I've consistently heard that BMW rallies are well-done, and my expectations for this one were high. I could smell the wealth in the room. At one point, I turned to Mike.

"I think our net worth is on the low side of average here."

Mike shook his head. "You're probably right."

At lunch, we sat with strangers: Zach from Birmingham (two hours south of where we call home), and Steve from Denver.

Steve was a BMW motorcycle encyclopedia of knowledge, and I enjoyed asking him questions about different BMW products.

After lunch, Steve approached Mike and me.

"Hey, if you guys come back through Denver, you're
welcome to stay at my place. I won't be in town,
but I can tell you where the key is hidden."

We thanked Steve for his offer but told him our current route took us through Colorado Springs south of Denver.

"If your plans change, just give me a call."

He wrote his cell number on a napkin and handed it to Mike.

If you don't ride a motorcycle, Steve's offer for two strangers to stay at his place probably sounds crazy. The riding community is amazing, and Steve's hospitality reminded us of that.

The Vendors

Hundreds of vendors were on-site, selling anything you can imagine. Mike purchased a BMW shirt and a couple of small items.

I purchased Moto-Skiveez padded underwear.

I told the owner (and inventor) that I would track him down and hug him if his product gave my backside relief.

He paused, then gave me a look as if to say …

"No need to do that, buddy."

Point taken.

I left on this adventure without a tank bag but hoped to find one today. I visited the Touratech and Givi booths, but neither had one with them that fit my GS.

Mike and I also talked to every vendor we could find that makes custom seats for the GS. There were more than a handful—probably because the stock seat on the GS needs improvement. Unfortunately, we didn't find what we were looking for.

No seat. No tank bag. I was disappointed.

Parking Lot Entertainment

Another highlight for me was watching a professional stunt rider perform tricks on stock BMW motorcycles in a barricaded area of the parking lot. From wheelies to front-tire stoppies to burn-outs, this guy could make the big BMWs do things that appeared to defy physics.

I was so mesmerized that I went back and saw the same show three hours later. I love the smell of burning rubber and brake dust. I guess I'm weird like that.

I skipped the rally closing ceremony and headed back to the hotel to rest and write this daily ride report. Actually, I wrote two. Yesterday was too long to write last night.

Mike stayed in the hope of winning a door prize. He texted me a little later and said he didn't win anything. I was a bit surprised. He usually does well in those sorts of things.

Final Thoughts

We ate dinner at a pizza place within walking distance. My riding gear appreciates the breather. Then I took a shower and washed my riding shirt for tomorrow.

It was great to be off my bike for a day.

Good for the body. Good for the soul.

Tomorrow, we're camping for the first time. I hope I brought everything. I don't have the guts to ask Mike if he'd share a spot in his tent.

States Traveled: Montana
Miles Ridden: 0.0

Reflections One Year Later

I think most people have the wrong idea about motorcycle rallies. Sure, some are centered around wet T-shirt contests and games to see who can drink the fastest through a funnel.

But most bike rallies aren't like that. Instead, they're about spending time with people who share the same passions.

Everyone I saw at the rally looked happy.

Our rest day in Billings was incredible, and it was nice to have control over my schedule. I preferred spending a few extra minutes relaxing and catching up on my journaling in the hotel, and Mike preferred spending his extra time hanging out in the vendor area.

We spent most of the day together, but for the first time since home (if you don't count St. Louis), we existed more than a few feet apart from one another.

I felt recharged and ready for the next leg of the journey.

Looking back, this BMW rally lived up to the hype. It was packed with interesting speakers, knowledgeable vendors willing to answer questions, better than average food, and participants who were passionate about the sport of motorcycling.

I wonder how Sturgis compares to this.

I could speculate, but I won't.

Beginning of Ride Day Four

Zach and Steve at BMW Rally

Moto-Skiveez Padded Underwear

Didn't Know My Bike Could Do That

Second Leg

Billings, Montana to Hyder, Alaska

This leg of our journey was totally different than the first. We took smaller roads, which allowed us to connect with our surroundings more intimately—*and we started to disconnect from our real lives.*

Each day revealed something new for us to learn—about Mother Nature, about life, about ourselves.

Montana, Wyoming, Alberta, British Columbia, and Alaska

FOURTEEN

Life Insurance

FLASHBACK: *Several weeks before departure ...*

We're supposed to leave in a few weeks, and Sue is getting nervous about the trip.

At dinner tonight, she asked detailed questions about my life insurance policy.

"Where is it? How much is it for?"

When I reminded her of the policy value, I noticed a slight twinkle in her eyes. I quickly informed her that it wasn't as much as it seemed since she would no longer be drawing my salary.

"Sue, if something happens to me, sell the house, simplify your spending, and you should be fine."

"But I don't want anything bad to happen to you."

I assured her that I wouldn't go on this trip if I thought there was even a ten percent chance of something happening to me.

She looked me square in the eyes.

"You know the chances are higher than that."

Reflections One Year Later

I'm not an idiot. I knew something could go wrong.

But it's also true that I could have a heart attack before I finish writing this sentence.

I weighed the risks of going and decided it was worth it. That's not to say I would come to the same conclusion ten years in the past or ten years into the future.

Life is fragile, but it cries out to be lived.

Several weeks before we left, I saw a wreck on the way to work where the driver lost control and crashed into a tree.

He died on impact.

He lost his life on the way to his j-o-b.

A yellow caution tape "POLICE LINE—DO NOT CROSS" circled the area for weeks as a reminder.

One year later, family members still keep fresh flowers around the trunk of the tree. I intentionally notice every morning.

Sometimes, I wonder if the man had a DREAM left undone.

I'm afraid we all do.

FIFTEEN

Ride Day Five

BEARTOOTH HIGHWAY

Sunday
Billings, Montana to Livingston, Montana

I felt much better after a day of rest.

Today was about three things: riding Beartooth Highway (a top ten motorcycle road), riding through Yellowstone, and tent camping for the first time.

After a decent continental breakfast, we loaded our gear, said goodbye to riders leaving at the same time, and headed southwest out of Billings on Highway 212—away from Alaska.

Good roads demand detours.

Mike's GS has been leaking oil since Alabama. From the smell, oil is leaking onto the exhaust pipe. It's been particularly pleasant for me since I've been riding behind him for most of the trip.

He had the oil changed before we left, and we suspect that the technician didn't tighten the oil filter properly.

This confirms my belief that you should never go on a trip immediately after having a vehicle serviced because service technicians often mess up one thing when fixing another.

But that's just a theory.

We wanted to enjoy the day without looking for fuel, so we stopped to top off our tanks about 75 miles into our ride.

We weren't the only riders from the BMW rally filling up.

I overheard one rider say to another.

"It's 45 degrees at the top of Beartooth Highway."

When we got back to our bikes, I told Mike what I had heard. We both added a rain liner to keep the wind out.

Beartooth Highway

When we pulled out, my GS showed 85 degrees Fahrenheit. It was hotter than that inside my steamy riding jacket.

I chose hot now so I could be comfortable later.

In no time, a sign reading "Beartooth Scenic Byway" signaled we were there. I was excited.

This was our first detour to ride a road we'd read about.

Almost instantly, the gloomy morning turned into a perfect day. The sky was a deep blue, and clouds were puffy white.

If I had one word to describe Beartooth Highway, it would be "switchbacks." They were fun to ride and equally fun to photograph. As we climbed, I could feel the temperature dropping.

Mike thought it was neat too.

"Hey Dave, if you want to stop, just let me know."

We stopped a bunch, and each one was worth the investment. Strangers offered to take our picture, and we reciprocated.

I was mesmerized by the entire ride. Each switchback revealed a fresh perspective of the mountain above and the valley below.

I imagine that Mike was getting tired of hearing me say "wow" inside his helmet. But I couldn't help myself. Today was a spectacular day to be riding a top ten motorcycle road.

At the highest elevation, Mike's GPS signaled 10,900 feet.

Neither motorcycle minded the altitude. It was 52 degrees.

On the way down, we stopped for a snack, then continued on Highway 212 toward Yellowstone National Park.

Yellowstone

Of all the destinations on our trip, Sue was most silent when I told her we were riding through Yellowstone.

She's wanted to go for years.

I thought about her as we got closer to the entrance.

I felt guilty that I was doing this without her.

The line to enter the park was long and slow. We barely moved for the next hour. Since our GSs are air-cooled, we started getting nervous they were overheating. We could smell something burning. We just couldn't tell for sure if it was Mike's bike leaking oil or both bikes overheating.

I hoped it was Mike's bike leaking oil.

We finally made it into the park, and within a few miles, we were greeted with spectacular views of Mother Nature.

Mike wanted to see Old Faithful, but the delay getting into the park cut into our plan. I was surprised at what Mike said next.

"Dave, since this is our first camping night, I think we should skip Old Faithful so we can make it to our campsite before dark."

I knew this part was important to him.

"Are you sure? I don't mind pushing through."

"Yes."

At the next turn, we took Highway 89 heading north.

We barely saw Yellowstone—hardly enough to say we had even been there. But I saw enough to want to go back.

Final Destination

Sixty miles later (before dark), we pulled into the Paradise Valley KOA campground near Livingston, Montana.

It is nicer than I expected.

After we checked in and found our site, I nervously opened the big black dry bag that had been strapped on the seat behind me for the last 2,000 miles.

That's where I packed all my camping gear.

Mike is a Boy Scout Leader with Wood Badge credentials—the highest level for a Scout Leader. I Googled it.

He showed me the best spot to pitch my tent. I had it up in no time. What a relief.

The Wood Badge on the team was point for building our first fire. Mike arranged the firewood we purchased at the campground store into a teepee shape with smaller pieces on the bottom.

I knew that much.

Then he walked over to his motorcycle and pulled out something from a plastic bag that looked like lint from a clothes dryer and placed it underneath the pile.

Flick. Flick. Flick. Nothing.

Does it say somewhere in the Wood Badge manual that you have to use flint to start a fire? I wondered.

"Hey Mike, I've got a lighter."

"I've got it," he replied.

Flick. Flick. Flick.

Finally, the blue-colored lint ignited and caught the small pile of kindling on fire. In no time, the fire was burning hard enough for us to know it wasn't going out.

The flint thing worked, but I found myself asking.

When did it become easier to bring dryer lint and a flint stick than bringing a lighter?

Does using flint make you more of a man?

Wouldn't a *real* man make fire by rubbing sticks together?

We took a shower (not together), then met back around the fire for our first dehydrated meal of the trip.

Mike brought his Jetboil, so heating water was a snap.

Just pour boiling water into the dehydrated food pouch, and ten minutes later, we had a gourmet meal—or something like it. I had beef stroganoff. Mike had chicken and rice. We tasted each other's meals and agreed that both were surprisingly good.

About the time we had finished eating, a man on a Goldwing pulled into the campsite next to us pulling something. It was too dark to know for sure, but it looked like a popup trailer.

He backed the trailer into the slot and unhooked it.

I whispered to Mike.

"If that thing has air conditioning, I'm going to be jealous."

The man proceeded to reconfigure his trailer into a one-person RV—like one of the transformer toys my son used to play with. Minutes later, I heard the hum of an air conditioner.

That must be nice, I thought.

After dinner, we sat around the fire in our Kermit chairs and enjoyed the calm of the evening. But the calm didn't last. Mike pulled up the weather radar on his phone.

"Dave, it's about to rain on us, now!"

We scurried to put everything in a dry spot and dashed into our separate tents right as it started pouring.

Final Thoughts

I'm sitting in my tent writing this ride report.

I sure hope she doesn't leak on my laptop. Tomorrow *should* be our last day in the United States. I'm nervous. I've never ridden a motorcycle anywhere else.

States Traveled: Montana and Wyoming
Miles Ridden: 260.1

Backstory

Mike hasn't always been the camping type. In fact, he once told me when his kids were young that he would never camp for more than one night at a time. As he explained it:

"I don't do campground showers."

I'm not sure what happened to *that* Mike, but the one sleeping in the tent next to mine is different. Mike is now knee-deep in the Boy Scouts. He's a Wood Badge, which means he did a lot of stuff proving he knows what he's doing outdoors.

I attended the ceremony where he was awarded the honor.

I'm not exactly sure what a Wood Badge is, but the ceremony made it look like a pretty big deal.

I remind him from time to time how his camping skills have evolved. He just rolls his eyes. If you haven't picked up on this habit, Mike likes to roll his eyes at me when I say something he doesn't agree with.

That's why I keep saying things I know he won't agree with.

I hope that doesn't make me a bad person.

Reflections One Year Later

David's Thoughts

Reading back through my ride reports, I can tell I was starting to relax and disconnect from thoughts about work—in a good way.

I always assumed Mike's GS electronics package (newer model) was more accurate than mine, but I certainly never admitted that to him. When our bikes disagreed on the ambient temperature, I always played like mine was correct, and his was off by a little.

Beartooth Highway was a high point for me. What started off as a dreary morning turned into a magnificent day as we headed higher along the switchbacks.

The views were spectacular.

We were hot at the bottom of the mountain and cold up top.

That's how it sometimes is when you're on a motorcycle.

As it turns out, our first campsite was the most picturesque of the trip, to me. It overlooked a meadow filled with cattle and dark green grasses. Mountains framed the backdrop at a distance.

Mike's original plan had us camping before Ride Day Five, but the delay in leaving forced us to ride farther each day, so we opted to stay in hotels. A wise decision.

My Kermit chair was a wonderful last-minute purchase before the trip. These chairs are comfortable and store in a very compact bag. They are too heavy to be good for hiking but well worth the expense and storage space on a motorcycle. Having a comfortable chair made camping enjoyable—at least on this night.

Sue and Drew went to Yellowstone one year after our trip. I couldn't go because of work. Maddie couldn't either. In hindsight, I wish Mike and I had spent more time there.

Sorry, Mike.

MIKE'S THOUGHTS

Beartooth Highway had been on my bucket list for some time.

The ride was everything I had imagined.

The road was curvy, narrow, and technical. I spent too much time watching the asphalt instead of enjoying the vista.

My only disappointment was how crowded it was.

The ride felt like a parade of Goldwings, Harleys, and BMWs. All three bike associations had a rally in the area that week or the following week.

The ride into Yellowstone was breathtaking, with the massive canyon walls, trout streams, and countless bison.

I wish we could have seen more.

Beginning of Ride Day Five

Gearing Up for the Elevation Change

Beartooth Highway

Higher Elevation Along Beartooth Highway

Flick. Flick. Flick

Our First Night Camping

SIXTEEN

Keeping Privates Dry

A PRODUCT WORTHY OF YOUR CONSIDERATION

What I'm about to tell you feels awkward.
I thought about deleting it from the final manuscript (more than once), but I didn't because it's too important.

Here goes ...

I'd like to recommend a product all riders (male and female) should consider when riding long distances.

My mentors told me about it. Now, I'm telling you.

It's called *Monkey Butt Powder*. Yep, that's the actual name. It's an anti-moisture, anti-friction product you apply "down there" to keep your "hardware" dry as a desert in a drought.

It's particularly important when you're riding in hot weather, but the anti-friction advantages are real in all weather conditions. Simply put, it does what it's advertised to do.

I just wish it could help with the trauma-like pain I'm experiencing "down there" from sitting on the seat from hell.

Wait. I said I wouldn't complain about my butt pain anymore.

Sorry.

Monkey Butt Powder

SEVENTEEN

Ride Day Six

TROUBLE

MONDAY
LIVINGSTON, MONTANA TO GREAT FALLS, MONTANA

It rained hard most of the night, and even though my tent is made for two, it was crowded in there with all my riding gear.

Considering this was our first camping night, I think things went well. At least I didn't forget something and have to ask Mike to make room. That would have been awkward.

Ron From Mississippi

The person who came in last night pulling a trailer was a friendly guy from Mississippi. Sure, I was a little jealous hearing his air conditioner running through the night, but I got over it.

Ron walked over this morning to introduce himself and offer us a cup of freshly brewed coffee. I felt joy.

Mike doesn't like coffee—which meant I could have two cups.

Ron was a jewel. He called his wife every hour or so and talked to her on speakerphone. I could tell she was worried.

Ron is a member of a Christian Motorcycle Group and on his way to Sturgis. He told us that a riding buddy was planning on coming with him but had to back out at the last minute.

He seemed excited (and nervous) about sharing his faith.

"I've always wanted to go there," he said, "but I couldn't when I worked full-time. I retired earlier this year, so here I am."

I asked Ron what his wife thought about his trip.

"She's worried. That's why I call her so often."

It turns out that Ron just retired from NASA's Stennis Space Center in Mississippi, a cousin to the NASA center where Mike and I work in Alabama.

We instantly felt like friends once we made the connection.

While we were packing up, Mike checked the weather radar and noticed it was raining to our north in the direction we were going. A few minutes later, Ron walked over.

"It looks like there's rain where you guys are heading."

We had known Ron for less than an hour, but it felt like he was genuinely worried about us. We told him we were prepared.

At least, we thought we were.

We spoke with Ron for a few more minutes, wished each other well, and then he asked if he could pray for us. We stood in a circle with our arms on each other's shoulders as Ron said a special prayer for our safety.

I was moved and fought back tears.

This was a special moment for me, and I'm sure for Mike too. A man we had just met only a few hours ago at a campground in Montana was praying for us.

Camping helps people connect.

So do motorcycles.

We had both.

Toward Alaska

Our destination for the evening was 350 miles away.

This should be a pretty easy day, I thought.

We made a final check to make sure our gear was strapped on tight, waved goodbye to Ron, and pulled out into clear blue skies. A few miles later, we turned onto Highway 89 heading north.

The first ten miles of our trip along the Yellowstone River were spectacular. We stopped once to take a photo, then pressed on.

Twenty miles later, Mike's GPS signaled that rain was ahead, so we pulled over and put on our light rain gear.

As we continued, the sky ahead turned darker and darker. We pulled over again—this time putting on all the rain gear we had brought. I put on my waterproof gloves and my rain pants/jacket that goes over my gear. I made sure both side cases were secure and put my phone and wallet in plastic bags.

Mike zipped his rain liner to the inside of his jacket.

Trouble

As we continued north, what started as a light drizzle turned into a heavy downpour. We kept riding.

Both of us were unusually silent.

The temperature dropped to 44 degrees. I was cold.

After riding in heavy rain for an hour and a half in the middle of nowhere, Mike said something that surprised me.

"Dave, I'm struggling."

Mike's tone alarmed me, and I immediately started looking for a place to pull off. Even small towns out here are sparse and separated by more distance than I'm accustomed to.

We finally found a rest area (the best we could do) and turned in. We pulled the GSs onto a small picnic area with a roof.

At least we were out of the miserable rain.

When Mike took off his helmet, I could see he was in trouble. He looked dazed. His rain liner had been leaking, and he was dripping wet. His pants were soaked.

He took off his left boot and poured water out.

I'd never seen him like this and realized he was on the edge of hypothermia. We were both shivering, but he was worse.

I wonder if this is how homeless people feel when it rains.

We were only 110 miles from where we started the day, but we both realized we needed to hit the abort button.

I suggested we find a hotel in the next town.

We hated the idea but knew this was our best option.

For the first time on our adventure, Mike had phone service when I didn't. After he warmed up and dried off a bit, he booked a hotel in Great Falls, Montana 50 miles away.

The idea of riding 50 miles in this mess nearly freaked me out. I knew it was going to be harder for Mike. A few minutes later, we left the protection of our pavilion and continued in the cold rain.

I took the lead and counted down the miles over the headset.

"Mike, we have 49 miles to go. We have 48 miles ..."

Fifty miles seemed like hundreds.

Final Destination

I've never been so happy to find our hotel. From the stares of the ladies at the check-in desk, we must have looked rough.

Either that—or they thought we were smoking hot.

I checked us in and jokingly asked if they had hot water. My question seemed to break the tension of our appearance.

They laughed. We took our stuff up.

I told Mike he had first dibs on a shower.

"Thanks, Dave."

A Shipment Home

My perfect packing job on Ride Day One isn't so perfect anymore. Packing is starting to feel like a calculus exercise.

I spotted an Office Depot near our hotel when we pulled in. By the time we finished checking in, I had a mental list of stuff I could survive without. I had a real pile of stuff in no time.

After both of us had showered (again, not together), we walked to Office Depot to make the shipment. Mike tossed a couple of small items into my backpack full of unnecessary crap.

When the salesperson handed me a receipt, I felt an immediate sense of relief—almost like a burden had been lifted.

Life looked better than it did three hours ago.

We walked to Chili's for dinner, then spent the evening drying gear and washing clothes.

Final Thoughts

I'm in the hotel lobby writing this ride report. I love this place and secretly wish we could stay another day—or two.

Today was far from a bust. We learned that Mike needs better rain gear and that I don't need 21 pairs of underwear.

Who knew they had washing machines out west?

I also learned that my mother-in-law worked in Yellowstone for two summers when she was in college.

I probably should have known that already.

In the end, we made the right call to abort the day.

States Traveled: Montana
Miles Ridden: 160.2

Reflections One Year Later

David's Thoughts

Waking to a Montana sunrise after our first-night camping was an amazing moment for me. Our campsite backed up to a field filled with sun, blue skies, and rolling hills. Spectacular.

Our struggles on this day were worse than I originally shared. When I pulled out my camera to capture Mike's hypothermia—I was in charge of photography, remember—he gave me a stern look of disapproval.

"David, I don't want my picture taken right now."

I put my camera away and realized the severity of the situation.

If you've ever ridden wet, you know that hypothermia can take hold in a flash. I was cold—and only my hands and feet were wet. Mike was pretty much dripping wet.

I can only imagine how he felt.

We were in an unfamiliar place on the edge of being in real trouble. I knew we had everything we needed to survive overnight if we had to: camping gear, a lighter (screw the flint stick), and dry stuff to burn to get a fire started.

But we both wanted the comfort of indoors.

Every mile to Great Falls was tough, but we clicked them off one by one. Every few minutes, one of us asked the other if he was okay. The headsets were magic. I can still remember how happy I felt when we pulled into the hotel parking lot.

We lost part of a ride day, but that didn't matter.

We were safe, and I was thankful we'd overcome the obstacle. The simple things in life are oftentimes the real treasures. We were humbled by the experience—and more confident we could handle what might happen next.

MIKE'S THOUGHTS

Have you ever had one of those "Oh crap" moments?

When we left our campsite, it was a beautiful day. A few miles later, dark clouds developed to our north.

The temperature began dropping. Rain was inevitable.

The only question in my mind was how wet will I get?

While packing my bike, I forgot to include my rain suit. I realized this on the first day but figured I would be okay.

I had the rain liner for my Olympia jacket, and on a normal summer day, the liner would have been enough.

This wasn't a normal summer day.

David and I began the long, slow ascent into the Lewis and Clark National Forest to around 8,000 feet. When we reached the Showdown Montana ski resort, it started drizzling.

We pulled over and put on our rain gear.

The rain became more intense with every mile. My jacket and pants were saturated as the temperature dropped into the mid-40s. I turned my GS hand warmers to full heat, but it wasn't enough. I started looking for a place to pull over, but there wasn't one.

Nothing.

My feet were soaked as my water-drenched pants guided water into my boots. My rain-proof gloves were rain-proof no longer.

My helmet was fogging as I struggled to stay focused.

I could tell I was getting hypothermic.

David and I didn't talk much. I didn't know how he felt, but I figured he couldn't be worse than I was.

Finally, a picnic area appeared on our right. David and I pulled our bikes under a pavilion large enough for one picnic table. We pushed the table to the side so our bikes would fit.

I was mentally exhausted and physically incapacitated.

I was struggling.

David wasn't hurting as much as I was because he pulled out his camera and started taking pictures of me. When I bluntly put a stop to it, I think he realized how bad off I was.

I opened my top case and pulled out a drying towel. It felt like a heating blanket compared to my wet gear. I took off my boots and poured out a pint of water from each.

Looking back, I'm not sure why I didn't make hot chocolate.

I don't think my mind was functioning normally.

After we collected our thoughts, we decided to do an abort for the day. We were about an hour out from Great Falls, Montana.

My phone had service, so I booked a room.

All we had to do was ride another 50 miles in the rain, cold, and road construction. David led the way and clicked through the miles over the headset.

Every mile was tough.

When we arrived, David checked us in, and I took a shower.

I can still remember how good the hot water felt.

Day Six Started with a Beautiful Sunrise

Ron from Mississippi

So Far So Good

Regrouping Under Pavilion in Lewis
and Clark National Forest

Happy to Make It to Great Falls, Montana

I Brought This Much Too Much

Shipping Extras Home

EIGHTEEN

Helmet Communications

FLASHBACK: *One month before departure ...*

It's one month before we're supposed to leave, and Mike thinks we should get helmet headsets so we can talk while we ride.

I'm not so sure.

Something magical happens when I put on a helmet.

I think more clearly, and I see the world around me differently. Maybe it's because I can't hear my phone ring or respond to a text. For a moment, I'm disconnected from my real life and connected to Mother Nature.

I'd prefer not to say for sure, but I *might* talk to myself when I'm all alone in there.

I'm apprehensive.

I don't want Mike to hear what I'm thinking.

As far as he knows, I'm somewhat normal—no need to reveal anything different at this stage in our friendship.

But Mike's right. Our adventure will be easier if we can talk on the way. I told him I would pay my part of whatever he picks out.

NINETEEN

Ride Day Seven

BORDER CROSSING

TUESDAY

GREAT FALLS, MONTANA TO RADIUM HOT SPRINGS, BC

C amp a night or two, or ride a motorcycle with wet gear, and
you'll appreciate the comfort of an above average hotel. The
Hilton Garden Inn was certainly that.

I hated to leave.

Packing without the stuff I sent home yesterday was a joy.

Today was about crossing into Canada and making up for lost
miles. We ate a CLIF Bar and hit the road early.

From Great Falls, we headed north on I-15.

I enjoyed the simplicity of riding on an interstate again.

Mike's original route had us riding Going-to-the-Sun Road in
Glacier National Park, but the road was closed due to wildfires.

Sixty miles later, just north of Conrad, Montana, we exited
and turned onto Highway 44 heading west. Thirty-five miles after
that, we turned right onto Highway 89 heading north again.

We stopped several times along the way to take pictures and
absorb the beauty of our surroundings.

I wonder if people who live here take all this for granted?

We saw a group of helicopter tankers being filled with water and fire retardant in a field just off the highway to our left.

I expected to smell smoke from the wildfires but didn't.

In fact, the sky was a noteworthy blue color—so intense that Mike and I discussed it in our helmets.

Chief Mountain

A few miles later, we turned left onto Highway 177 and weaved our way along the two-lane road. We could see Chief Mountain to our left at a distance. It became more impressive as we continued —just like the Gateway Arch in St. Louis.

We were within 15 miles of the Canadian border, but this was too beautiful to rush. We stopped several more times, and each revealed a different viewpoint.

We lost sight of Chief Mountain from time to time, but that was fine because we needed to concentrate on riding. We rounded one corner and found a trail of animal droppings littering the road. Either cattle cross here, or it's one hell of a deer crossing.

I suppose a head-on collision with a truck would be worse, but the idea of going down on a road full of dung sounds like a close second. Maneuvering around the slippery mess required disciplined concentration, but we made it.

Funny story averted.

Trees blocked our view, and we lost sight of Chief Mountain for a good while. All the sudden, we rounded a corner, and there it was again, perfectly framed against the blue sky. It looked different than it did a few minutes ago. Much different.

Breathtaking!

Simply Wow

Without saying a word, we pulled over, dismounted our motorcycles, and stood there in awe. I flipped up my visor to make sure the tinted shield wasn't making it prettier than it really was.

After a minute or so, Mike broke the silence.

"Dave, I don't have the vocabulary to describe this."

His words rang true. The only thing I could say was, "wow." At that moment, I knew I was seeing something I'd never be able to fully describe in words or pictures—even here.

We hardly spoke while we were stopped. We didn't need to.

It was apparent from our silence that we were thinking the same thing. We stayed as long as we could, but we had a border to cross. Riding 400+ miles in a day takes discipline.

Into Canada

As we neared the border, I became apprehensive. I'd never crossed into another country on a motorcycle.

Would the border guard look inside my bags?

Would I have to show my registration and proof of insurance?

By chance, we pulled in line behind a guy on a Goldwing. Good, we can get a quick look at what to expect.

The guard looked at the rider's passport, talked to him for a minute or so, then motioned him through. Mike was next.

Mike pulled up to the gate and handed the guard his passport. Then he took off his helmet. I removed my helmet and waited my turn. Moments later, Mike pulled away.

Canada let Mike in. I was next. I proceeded to the gate.

"Passport, please," the border guard said.

I took out my passport and handed it to him.

"You going to the same place he is?"

"Yes, sir."

"Have you ever been to Canada?"

"Yes, to Niagara Falls and the Toronto area."

Aside: Do border guards have to pay a fine if they smile?

He scanned my passport, paused to make sure the computer was okay with me entering, then handed it back.

"Welcome to Canada, Mr. Mixson."

"Thank you, sir."

I put my passport in my pocket and my helmet on my head.

I pulled up to where Mike was waiting 50 yards ahead and tightened my helmet strap.

"Mike, we made it through!"

Relieved

Both of us were inside Canada, and I couldn't help but smile. For some reason, this border crossing was always a hurdle in my mind. So many things *could* have happened.

What if one of us misplaced our passport?

What if there's another David Mixson who's bad?

What if Mike has a shady past I don't know about?

Just because we've been friends for more than 20 years doesn't mean I really know him. I've seen this sort of thing on TV more than once. Do they arrest people when they attempt to cross into Canada with a record?

We left the United States on Highway 17 and entered Canada on Highway 6. We didn't make it more than two miles before I called for a photo stop.

It was that good.

The Rocky Mountains bordered us to our left for what seemed like forever. We weaved our way through them. The temp dropped to 52 degrees Fahrenheit as we did.

Fifty miles into Canada, we stopped for fuel in Pincher Creek, Alberta and filled up with liters instead of gallons. My tank was more than half-full, but I liked the idea of being able to make it back to my home country if my credit card was declined.

You never know.

When I started my GS back, a "failed light" warning came on.

"Mike, is my headlight on? I think it just blew."

"Nope. It's not on."

Sure enough, the GS computer was right. I wanted to bring a spare bulb, but it never made it high enough on my To-Do List.

Mike's bike is leaking oil, and mine is missing a headlight.

We stopped for lunch at A&W, and I used my phone to check which bulb I needed. I was afraid it would require a special BMW product, but a common headlight bulb (H7) was good enough.

Walmart in Canada

I searched for an auto parts place nearby but found a Walmart. I had never been so happy to see one in my life.

Actually, I had never been happy to see a Walmart, until then.

I rode over and bought an H7 bulb (two of them, in fact). I also bought a wrench so we can remove the skid plate on Mike's bike to see where the oil is leaking.

While I was there, I visited an ATM. I like knowing I have enough Canadian cash to make it back to my country.

From Pincher Creek, we took Highway 3 heading west. Forty miles later, we crossed from Alberta into British Columbia, and in another forty miles, we turned onto Highway 93 for a piece, then onto Highway 95 heading north.

We didn't stop much to take pictures because we're camping tonight and wanted to pitch our tents in light. Also a factor, my only working low beam bulb was in my side case.

Not long past Walmart, we remembered we needed another bottle of fuel for Mike's Jetboil. We drove through several small towns throughout the day looking for a resupply. No luck.

Final Destination

Our final destination for the evening is the Canyon Campground in Radium Hot Springs, British Columbia. We barely made it here before dark. The campsite store was closing when we arrived.

We checked in, pitched our tents, and rode to a German place we noticed on the way in. After dinner, I told Mike it was the best German food I'd eaten in years—because it's the *only* German food I'd eaten in years.

We rode back to the campsite and decided to keep the evening simple. Mike hung a battery-powered light from a tree limb, and we talked about our first day in Canada.

Final Thoughts

I'm sitting in my tent writing this ride report. It's not raining at the moment, but it has been. Everything is wet—and it's cold. I'm glad I bought the 15-degree sleeping bag instead of the 45.

Places Traveled: Montana, Alberta, and British Columbia
Miles Ridden: 464.4

Reflections One Year Later

Mike was leading when we ran into the patch of cow dung.
"Dave, be careful. There's crap in the road."

I slowed down and dodged as much of it as I could, hoping I wouldn't have to make this call home.

"Sue, I crashed on a slippery patch of cow poop."

Stopping at Chief Mountain was one of the most memorable moments of the trip for me. It ranks as one of the most majestic things I've seen in my life.

I doubt it always looks this way, but at that moment, it did.

I wish I could describe the experience with words. But I can't. The pictures we took look great, but they fall short of capturing what we saw. That's why I'm not publishing them here or online.

Mike and I are the only ones who know how it was.

When we made it into Canada, I felt a huge sense of relief. When the border guard asked me if I'd been to Canada, I forgot to mention that Sue and I celebrated our honeymoon in Victoria, British Columbia back in 1990—over half my life ago.

Maybe the dementia is already setting in.

Beginning of Ride Day Seven

Fourteen Miles From Canada

Border Crossing Into Canada—Taking the Lead
Photographer Job Seriously

First Photos of Bikes in Canada

Hello Alberta Canada

Campsite in Radium Hot Springs, British
Columbia Canada

Writing Ride Report for the Day

TWENTY

Interstate Riding

STRAIGHT ROADS AREN'T SO BAD

I have a secret you might think is strange.

I enjoy riding on interstates.

Riding on an interstate takes less focus, less planning, and less defensive riding. The buzz of the engine and the sound of pavement rolling underneath puts my mind in a happy place.

On long open stretches, I let my mind go a bit and focus less on the mechanics of riding, and more on life and the beauty of Mother Nature around me.

I can do this because there aren't any stoplights or intersections or sharp curves—or cars wanting to turn left in front of me.

I enjoy being in the moment.

I wonder where the trucker I just passed is heading and how his life might be different, or the same, as mine.

I enjoy identifying parts of Mother Nature.

I enjoy the smell of freshly cut grass and newly plowed fields.

I enjoy making new goals for my life.

I enjoy studying how the draft from the 18-wheeler is going to bounce me around when I pass.

I enjoy the peace of not shifting.

Many of these sensory experiences lead me to my past.

The smell of freshly plowed dirt reminds me of visiting my grandparents' farm when I was a kid.

Sunrises remind me of a place I lived years ago that had the most wonderful view of the eastern sky. I woke up most mornings and enjoyed the sunrise like it was my last.

Sunsets remind me of being at the beach with my parents when they were still alive.

Motorcyclists are supposed to enjoy curvy roads the best, but there's a special place in my heart for a long stretch of interstate to clear my mind and soul.

Long straight roads make me happy.

Simple as that.

Mike on a Long Straight Road

TWENTY-ONE

Ride Day Eight

DENNIS

WEDNESDAY
RADIUM HOT SPRINGS, BC TO JASPER, ALBERTA

I t rained last night, and my tent is wet.

I worry about mildew, but the Wood Badge on the team says it *should* be fine as long as everything dries out in the next couple of days. I'm beginning to wonder if we'll ever be dry for more than a few hours.

Radium Hot Springs is a picturesque little town comprised of mom-and-pop-type businesses and surrounded by Mother Nature at its best. I didn't see any chain restaurants (besides Subway) and only a few modest hotels.

Maybe that's why Mike decided to camp here.

From our campsite, we turned left on Highway 93 heading northeast. A few miles later, the road ran between a gigantic rock formation in Sinclair Canyon.

I called for a photo stop and pulled over.

"Mike, this is too good to pass up. Ride ahead a bit, then turn around and ride back toward me, and I'll take your picture."

I pulled over and framed the perfect shot. Mike did as I asked, and I took several photos of him riding toward me heading southwest. As he rode by, I turned back and noticed that the view in the other direction was even better.

"Oh my gosh, Mike. The light is better the other way!"

Mike turned around (again) and rode back toward me heading northeast. I took a round of eight photos and called it a shoot.

"Was that good?" Mike said as he passed by.

"Yes. That was perfect. Just pull over and wait for me."

All this coordination was done with our headsets. When they work correctly, they're life-changing. It seems like they're working better and better as we go along—suggesting our earlier problems could have been user error.

Detour Ahead

Our distance for the day was relatively short (300 miles), so Mike suggested we take a detour to Banff, Alberta.

I agreed.

An hour later, we turned right onto Highway 1 heading southeast near Castle Junction. For the second time on this trip, we were riding away from Alaska.

We ran into rain a short time later and stopped to put on rain gear. Mike desperately needs something waterproof to put over his jacket. He gets wet when it rains more than a sprinkle.

I could tell he was getting frustrated.

Twenty-five miles later, we were in Banff. The best I could tell, Banff is an upscale tourist/ski town. Mike looked for rain gear and cooking fuel for his Jetboil, and I looked for a coffee shop.

I know that doesn't seem fair, but I'd been without good java since Alabama, and I saw several coffee shops on the drive through town that excited me. Mike understands my passion for coffee and knew where I was going before I told him—just as friends should.

We agreed on a meet-up time and place and then split up.

The first coffee shop I found was Evelyn's Coffee Bar. I ordered a latte and enjoyed a few moments of solitude.

Meanwhile, Mike found rainproof pants. Life is good.

When I found Mike, he was talking to another stranger. Mike enjoys sharing our trip with anyone who shows interest.

I don't recall him being this way in Alabama.

We ate a quick lunch at McDonald's then headed out feeling refreshed. I left with a latte in my stomach, and Mike left with rain gear. Nice detour.

More Rain

A few miles outside of town, we turned left back in the direction we had come. The next stretch of road between Banff and Jasper is known as the Icefields Parkway.

Ten miles later, we ran into more rain, so Mike started looking for a private place to change into his new waterproof pants.

The only spot he could find was the entrance to the Bourgeon Lake Trail. We turned in and parked. Mike grabbed some items from his side bags and started walking toward a small covered area where a map signaled the start of the hiking trail.

"Mike, are you sure you want to change pants in full view? The parking lot is full, and people could return at any moment."

"David, I don't care."

Mike stripped down to his briefs (didn't see that coming) and changed pants out in the open. I never imagined when we entered Canada that Mike might leave with a criminal record.

Fortunately, nobody came up while he was changing.

Great. I still have a navigator.

Mike doesn't get flustered, but he was more than sick and tired of being wet and cold. Riding with good rain gear can be aggravating. Riding with less-than-good rain gear can be dangerous.

We suited back up and headed out in the rain.

A few miles later, I asked.

"How are your new pants working?"

"So far, so good. At least my legs are dry."

Bow Lake

Near Lake Louise, we continued on the Icefields Parkway heading northwest toward Jasper, Alberta Canada—our camping destination for the evening. A short time later, the rain cleared, and the sky turned a magnificent blue.

We stopped to take off our rain gear and continued in awe.

Our path followed along the Bow River.

Sixty miles from lunch, we pulled over at Bow Lake.

It's hard to describe this moment. The sky was a deep blue, and the water was the most intense turquoise color I've ever seen.

A lake can't really be this color, can it?

It turns out that it can.

By now, I was starting to bore myself with "wow," and I know Mike must have been tired of hearing me say it in his helmet.

I warned him before we left that I talk to myself.

I took more than 20 pictures to make sure it was real. Then we continued toward Jasper.

Final Destination

We rode another 120 miles and arrived at Whistler's Campground in Jasper National Park with plenty of daylight left. I was excited. Provincial campgrounds in Canada are rumored to be nice.

We checked in and rode to our campsite.

Our site for the night is centrally located near the amenities and more open than the last two.

Even better, the ground is dry.

I pulled my tent out of the bag and poured water out. I put it up wet, and within a few hours, it was dry.

We are in bear country, and the campground attendant warned us to secure all food in the provided bear-proof storage lockers.

The closest one to our campsite is about 30 yards away.

Mike asked her if it would be safe to keep food in our motorcycle aluminum side cases.

"It *should* be fine," she said.

There's that "should" word again.

I opted to put my food in lockers made to keep large animals out. The idea of bears attacking my motorcycle doesn't interest me, even though it would make a cool picture.

Mike opted to use his motorcycle cases.

Once our campsite was set up, I took a shower at the men's bathhouse about 50 yards away and grabbed a load of firewood at the free woodpile on the way back.

When I got there, Mike was stacking kindling for the fire.

"Dave, can I borrow your lighter?"

"Sure, but I thought Wood Badges use flint."

Mike rolled his eyes without saying a word.

Headlight Repair

While Mike was building a fire, I decided to replace my headlight.

Online forums said the procedure was challenging because you have to "feel" your way through the changeout. I'm pretty handy but opted not to make the repair last night in the dark.

I figured I could survive using my high beam.

A bulb replacement at a campsite in Canada seemed far more complex than one in the comfort of my garage back home—especially since I haven't seen a single shop here to fix my screw-up.

The procedure was difficult and took me longer than it should have. But I was able to get the new bulb installed just fine. I'm not sure it's latched correctly, but it's working, and I'm happy with *good enough* until I get back home.

Just as I finished, a couple walked over and introduced themselves. John and Sherrie are from Denver, Colorado and own GSs. They weren't riding them but saw ours and stopped by.

Having the same motorcycle gave us an instant connection.

It's weird like that.

We talked for a while longer, then John wrote his cell number on a napkin and handed it to us.

"Call me if you have trouble on your way through Colorado."

Is everyone from Colorado friendly?

This is the second time that someone from there has given us their cell phone number. Remember Steve at the BMW rally?

Mike boiled water, and we made food in a pouch. Mike had red beans and rice. I had eggs and biscuits.

It sounds gross, but both meals were pretty tasty.

Then There Was Dennis

After dinner, a man riding a Harley pulled up to the empty tent in the camping spot next to us.

A few minutes later, he walked over and introduced himself.

Dennis is a retired steelworker from the Toronto area and had been touring western Canada for several weeks. He showed us a video on his phone of a bear he saw earlier in the week.

Dennis seemed happy.

Nearly two hours into our conversation, Dennis told us:

"I've tried to get into the United States several times, but the border guards won't let me in because I have a felony conviction."

Dennis stayed for a while longer, then walked back to his tent for the evening. We sat around the fire laughing about whether we should tell our wives about our new friend.

Final Thoughts

I'm inside my tent writing this ride report. I hope the noise I just heard isn't a bear. I doubt this tent would hold up to his claws.

Two more days of riding, and we'll be in Alaska. It's hard to imagine that we're not even halfway home yet. It's equally hard to imagine that we've ridden a motorcycle across the United States and into Canada—on the way to freaking Alaska.

We didn't ride very far today. I should feel rejuvenated, but I don't—probably because we had a lot of seat time for the miles. But trust me, the scenery was out-of-this-world beautiful.

It just doesn't stop. I didn't expect this.

Places Traveled: Alberta and British Columbia
Miles Ridden: 281.3

Reflections One Year Later

We were both getting tired of riding in the rain.

I didn't say much about it in the original ride reports because I didn't want people to say, "Gosh, your trip would have been great if it wouldn't have rained so much."

That, and because it sounds whiny to complain.

Banff was an interesting place, and I'm pretty sure we only saw a fraction of it. I can see myself going back with Sue.

An unexpected element of our adventure is that Mike was a stranger magnet. On numerous occasions, I had to pry him away from his new friends.

I just about fell over laughing when I saw him talking to Butch in Banff. The two of them carried on like they were old friends.

"Mike, do you know that guy?"

"Nope, just met him."

Campground facilities don't excite me, but the public shower at Whistler's is worthy of mentioning. It had hot water and private stalls—the two most important components of an above-average campground shower to a man my age.

The shower had one annoying feature, though, an automatic "off" valve that stopped water flow a few seconds after each push.

Push the button and bathe an arm.

Push the button and bathe the other arm.

I called for photo stops a lot. On several occasions, we stopped within 100 yards of our last.

Mike didn't complain a single time.

Choose wisely when you pick a friend to ride to Alaska with.

Three years later, the picture of Mike riding at Sinclair Canyon is still the background on my laptop computer.

Dennis was a character and made our time in Jasper memorable. I wasn't as excited about becoming friends as Mike was. His felony record was the first flag, and the fact that he discussed his crime so openly was the second.

And why was he traveling alone?

I came up with several snappy headlines for the nightly ride report but decided not to post them. I didn't want our wives back home to worry.

I was a little nervous about bears snooping around our stuff while we were sleeping. I could have had something stuck between my teeth. Plus, I'm certain I've eaten a CLIF Bar or two inside my tent on previous nights.

I thought about opening a CLIF Bar and rubbing it on the outside of Mike's tent but decided I needed a navigator.

In hindsight, maybe I should have tossed some food scraps by Dennis's tent—just to be on the safe side.

Beginning of Ride Day Eight

Sinclair Canyon

Stopping to Put on Rain Gear—Again

Banff, Alberta Canada

Mike Talking to Another Stranger

Mike Changes at Bourgeon Lake Trail

Bow Lake—Simply Amazing!

John and Sherrie From Denver

Hello British Columbia

TWENTY-TWO

Where You Headed?

MEETING STRANGERS ALONG THE WAY

I had no idea so many strangers would want to talk to two old guys riding motorcycles to Alaska.

We rarely stopped during the 21-day journey without someone approaching us to say hello and ask where we were going. Sure, we wore hi-vis yellow riding gear (which made us super easy to spot), but don't people know you're not supposed to talk to strangers?

I wonder if we would have been treated with the same warmness had we been wearing Harley leathers instead?

Meeting people was an unexpected treasure of the trip. I think the motorcycles made the difference. And the magnitude of gear strapped on the back signaled we were going somewhere big.

"Where you headed?" was the most common question—and the one I enjoyed answering the most.

"Alaska" always brought a smile.

"Wow, that sounds exciting."

As we got closer and closer, our answer sounded less impressive, so we followed it up with, "We started in Alabama."

This anchored our trip, regardless of where we were.

Strangers were extra nice when they saw us in the rain. Maybe I should have put a donation box on the back of Mike's bike.

TWENTY-THREE

Ride Day Nine

MORE CANADA

Thursday
Jasper, Alberta to Prince George, BC

Dennis walked over this morning to hang out with Mike.

If I was the jealous type, I'd think Dennis was trying to steal my riding partner and friend.

Within minutes, I overheard Mike giving Dennis his Facebook info. I was mortified because Mike links to my ride reports!

After what seemed like a very long time, Dennis said goodbye and wished us well. He didn't offer to pray for us like Ron did.

We didn't offer either. Opportunity lost.

When Dennis left, I told Mike about my concerns.

"We have to get out of here before Dennis reads what I wrote about him last night!"

I don't recall Mike's exact response, but we started loading up as fast as we could. We needed to leave before Dennis had a chance to mess up our adventure.

I glanced over and saw that Dennis was in his tent.

Was he reading my ride report?

All of the sudden, thoughts of his crime filled my mind.

Did he kill someone?

What kind of weapon did he use?

Did his victims die fast, or was it slow and painful?

I figured that our best defense was a good offense. I knew we could survive if we left first. Dennis can't follow us back into the United States, and he won't be able to catch us in Canada because he has to stop for gas more often than we do.

That's our GS advantage.

He's on a Harley.

Departure

We beat Dennis out of the campground and turned onto Highway 16 heading northwest.

The rain we were getting used to disappeared.

It was a beautiful morning.

Forty miles later, we stopped at Moose Lake.

Like Bow Lake, the water was a magnificent turquoise color. We paused to absorb the moment and to take pictures, then rode another 20 miles to Mount Robson Provincial Park.

Mount Robson was a popular spot. The parking lot was stuffed with RVs. Mike and I split up and walked around separately.

I bought a snack at the gift shop and sat under a huge cypress tree near our bikes. The air was crisp, and Mount Robson looked postcard-like in the distance.

For the first time in a long time, I didn't feel rushed.

I was happy gawking at the view and resting. I kept a close eye on the parking lot for Dennis, just in case.

One hour later, Mike walked up.

I'm not sure where he went (I didn't ask), but if there was a museum close by, I'm certain he devoured every fact.

I learned that about Mike at Mount Rushmore.

We chatted for a few minutes, then suited up and continued on Highway 16 heading northwest.

Where Did He Go?

One hundred miles later, Mike suggested we stop for a break at the Slim Creek Rest Area up ahead.

We turned in a few minutes later.

The area was picturesque. A creek (probably called Slim Creek) ran along the back of the property. I took off my gear and opened my side case for a drink.

When I looked up, Mike was gone.

The first thing that popped into my mind:

He's getting in the creek!

Like a father searches for his missing child, I started searching for Mike. I walked toward a clump of trees that blocked my view of the creek. As I got closer, I saw a pair of boots on the edge of the creek and a man-figure standing in the stream.

"Dude, what are you doing?" I asked.

"I told you I was going to get in a creek on this trip."

I pulled out my camera and took a handful of photos to fully capture the moment.

A 52-year-old man wearing a hi-vis yellow motorcycle jacket and a ball cap, with his pants rolled up, walking around in a creek in Canada.

He looked like a kid splashing in the rain for the first time.

A short time later, we put on our gear and continued northwest on Highway 16.

Then There Was Normal

It's hard to match the beauty we've seen over the last several days.

When we pulled into Prince George, British Columbia, Mike spoke in his helmet.

"Dave, this looks like home."

"I was thinking the same thing," I said.

Walmart was on our left, then a McDonald's, Home Depot, Michael's, and a Dairy Queen.

Are we really in Canada? According to Mike's GPS, yes.

Final Destination

Our camping spot for the night is the Blue Cedars Campground.

It's a dump.

Who would camp here when they could drive a few miles and camp in Mother Nature? My best guess: desperate riders on their way to Alaska, and people who need a cheap place to live.

Broken-down campers (some with blue tarps over their roofs) litter the campground. We're the only riders staying the night.

Heck. We might be the only ones who don't live here.

But all we need is a spot to pitch our tents. And for that, this place is good enough. I'm sure Mike can tell I'm not thrilled, but I didn't say anything because I didn't spend all the hours planning this like he did.

So what? We got a below-average campground.

It just makes the other places we've stayed seem nicer.

Bad things in life tend to do that.

Just in case you want to know, we set up our campsite in a tad over 24 minutes. We weren't in a hurry. I was just curious.

There aren't any restaurants within walking distance, so we rode to Mike's Steak House for dinner. How could we not?

The place felt comfortable, similar to a Chili's or an Outback back home, but different too.

After we ordered, I asked our server about the local industry.

"A lot of guys work in oilfields about three hours north."

I enjoyed dinner, in part, because it reminded me of home. We rode back to our campsite, built a fire, and relaxed. No one spoke to us except the campground staff.

I miss Dennis.

Even though this city reminds me of home, we are a long way from Alabama. My body knows it. My mind knows.

Final Thoughts

I'm sitting in my tent writing this ride report.

Today wasn't as rushed, and I feel more relaxed. I think Mike does too. We rode through some amazing scenery—and we didn't get wet. What's not to love about that?

The ride this morning was more of the same. The views of the Canadian Rockies to our left (west) were breathtaking.

I'm afraid part of me is starting to take all this for granted.

Incredible views are beginning to feel normal. I found myself comparing Mount Robson to Mount Rushmore, and Moose Lake to Bow Lake. This isn't what I want to do. I want to enjoy each stop in that moment. So what if Moose Lake wasn't as spectacular as Bow Lake. It was still incredible.

I think both of us are excited we've made it this far. I figure we can get a tow to Alaska if we have to, or at least hitch a ride—or pay for a very expensive taxi. We are close, and I can feel it.

Places Traveled: Alberta and British Columbia
Miles Ridden: 241.0

Reflections One Year Later

This ride day was rejuvenating. I had more energy at the end of the day than I did when we started. That's powerful.

You might have figured this out already, but the Blue Cedars Campground was my least favorite campground of the trip.

So far—that is.

We selected a spot as far from the dilapidated, tarp-covered RVs as we could. My plan to go unnoticed worked perfectly.

As we rode deeper into Canada, I became more apprehensive —probably because we were getting farther from help.

How many of my friends even have a passport?

Prince George felt like a real city instead of a tourist stop. It felt comfortable, familiar. People we ran into seemed friendly.

But no one asked us where we were going. I suspect we weren't the first to ride through on the way to Alaska.

Beginning of Ride Day Nine

Dennis Hanging Out With Mike

Moose Lake

Mount Robson

Mike Living a Dream

TWENTY-FOUR

What's Your Big Dream?

Quick break to ask you something.

What do you dream about doing but haven't?

If you're like me, you've made excuses of "why not" for far too long. Maybe your dream is to run a marathon, restore an old car, or hike the Appalachian Trail.

Maybe it's to backpack across Europe, participate in Running of the Bulls, or spend a month at the beach.

Only you can say—and there are no wrong answers.

Would you do something for me? Put this book down, close your eyes, and think about the answer to my question:

What do you dream about doing but haven't?

If you have more than one BIG DREAM, that's fine. I'll walk you through an exercise a little later in the book that will help you define and execute your BIG DREAM.

Go ahead. Take some time to answer my question. I'll wait.

WHAT DO YOU DREAM ABOUT DOING BUT HAVEN'T?

TWENTY-FIVE

Ride Day Ten

FINAL PUSH

Friday

Prince George, BC to Hyder, Alaska

Maybe my thoughts yesterday about being close enough for a tow were exaggerated. We still have a long day ahead of us before we can say we rode our motorcycles to Alaska.

I was excited and nervous at the same time.

We agreed at dinner last night to knock out 200 miles and stop for lunch in Smithers, BC.

This would be almost halfway to Alaska.

Per our standard operating procedure, we gassed up last night.

We left this morning earlier than we did most camping days because we wanted to arrive in Alaska with margin.

We packed up our tents, ate a CLIF Bar, then pulled out at 7:35 a.m. We continued on Highway 16 (our home since Jasper) heading west.

The computer on my GS said it was 43 degrees Fahrenheit.

On our way to Smithers, it started raining. We pulled off and put on our first layer of rain gear, hoping it would stop.

Instead, it continued to rain harder, so I told Mike I needed to pull over (again) and put on my full rain gear.

I was cold and uncomfortable. I knew Mike was worse.

Rain gear doesn't breathe, which makes it uncomfortable when it's hot. That's why we put it on in layers as we need it.

Mike's new pants work great, but he still needs something to put over his riding jacket to keep the water out—especially now that it's getting colder.

The cold and wet were starting to remind me of Ride Day Six. My GS signaled it was 48 degrees.

I didn't ask Mike what his said.

"Dave, I need to find a rainproof jacket. This isn't working."

"Let's take our time in Smithers and find you something,"

At this point, it didn't matter if it was for a motorcyclist.

Anything waterproof would be good enough. We made one quick photo stop and rode with purpose the rest of the morning.

Lunch

A little over 200 miles from breakfast, we arrived in Smithers. We were cold, wet, and dejected. Riding in the rain, even when you have the right gear, is mentally and physically exhausting.

In addition to the obvious discomfort of being cold and wet, there's less visibility to ride defensively and less friction to stop and make turns.

All this slows you down, which requires more seat time to travel the same number of miles. We were so close to our goal, but in many ways, Alaska felt so far away. Almost out of reach.

By Southern standards, Smithers looked pretty normal. Mike and I agreed it would easily pass for a small town in Alabama. We chose McDonald's because we were mentally drained and didn't want to spend time looking for something unique.

We were dripping wet and tried to shake off before we walked in. We must have looked rough based on the stares.

For the first time in my life, I ordered coffee with my Big Mac meal. Mike ordered hot chocolate with his.

We were cold and wet to the core.

While we were waiting for our food, I went to the restroom and put my riding gloves under the hand dryer to dry them out. I kept hitting the restart button, hoping not to blow a circuit.

For the umpteenth time on this trip, we looked pitiful. I guess we didn't seem very approachable because nobody said anything to us. Instead, the senior citizens there for discounted coffee stared at us like we didn't belong.

My order number 77 was ready a few minutes later.

Before I ate anything, I took the lid off my coffee and put my hands above it. I closed my eyes. The steam from the cup warmed my hands in an almost spiritual way. I carefully took a sip and felt the hot fluid warming my insides on the way down.

That was worth the price of the entire meal, I thought.

After we ate, Mike called several shops looking for a rain jacket large enough to fit over his riding jacket. He preferred one made for motorcyclists because they don't flap in the wind, but at this point, he didn't much care as long as it kept the rain out.

The best he could find was a shop close by that had a good selection of standard rain jackets in stock.

That was good enough.

Shopping and Coffee

The McDonald's was warm and dry, and I didn't want to leave.

But we had to if we wanted to make it to Alaska—the purpose of our trip. We put on our cold, wet riding gear and rode to the store Mike had called.

When we turned in, I spotted a coffee shop.

I think you can guess what happened next.

"Mike, I'm getting coffee. Come get me when you're done."

"Okay."

The coffee shop, Bugwood Bean, was really a coffee hut.

It didn't have inside seating, but that didn't matter because I was geared up. By now, it had stopped raining, and I was perfectly happy to enjoy a hot drink outside.

I walked up to the building and ordered a large latte.

The head barista completed my order and poured the last bit of foamed milk into a pattern on top. His pattern was a step above the latte art I had seen before. I added brown sugar (my preference when splurging) and took my first sip.

I've heard froth in a perfect latte described as silky smooth. After my first sip, I understood what that meant. The frothed milk on this latte was like a smooth buttery substance.

The espresso base was balanced and strong.

Like a fine wine compared to cheap, this was one of the best lattes I've ever had. Is cow's milk different in Canada?

For a moment, I thought about ordering another one, but I knew Mike would be back soon. I was also a little nervous the next one might not be as magical as the first.

I wanted to remember this as the best latte I'd ever had.

As I was taking my last sip, Mike walked up with a grin.

"I assume this means you found something."

He pulled out a normal-looking dark navy blue rain jacket from the bag.

"It's not perfect, but it *should* help."

There's that "should" word again.

We geared up and headed out.

Last Leg

According to Mike's GPS, we were 230 miles from Alaska.

Doable, but both of us were tired. Riding in gloomy weather takes more energy. I was thankful we got an early jump on the day.

It started raining again a few miles outside Smithers.

We pulled over and put on our full rain gear. This time, Mike had something to put over the outside of his normal riding jacket —an awkward-looking navy blue waterproof windbreaker.

It looked just like one I had in middle school, but I didn't say anything. I needed a happy navigator.

Eighty miles later (near Kitwanga, BC), we stopped for gas and to take pictures of a huge road sign that signaled we were close. The sign read "Hyder AK 240 km."

By my quick calculation, that's about 150 miles.

Engineering school pays off when you least expect it.

I took the lead and continued on Highway 37 heading north.

On this final push to Alaska, I couldn't help but think about what this trip means. Before we left, I imagined how I would feel when we crossed into Alaska. I always figured I would feel a sense of accomplishment but not overwhelming joy.

This trip was never about the destination.

Mike and I must have been thinking the same thing because we started talking about it inside our helmets.

"Mike, I don't plan on jumping up and down when we cross into Alaska."

"Me neither."

About 140 miles from Alaska it started raining harder. I slowed our pace. Now would be the worst time to crash, I thought.

The roads got smaller and slippery as we continued.

All of a sudden, my back tire slid out as I rounded a corner.

I shouted to Mike in my headset, warning him.

My heart raced. I knew that was a close call. I'm glad I didn't have to tell my friends back home that I *almost* made it to Alaska.

"Mike, I'm going to take it easy from here."

"I agree," he said.

It was overcast for the most part, but every once in a while, the clouds broke, and I could see blue and different shades of green. An occasional waterfall guided melting snow to the ground.

In a strange way, the overcast gray added a soothing contrast. It was almost like we were looking at a black and white photograph.

At one point, the sun poked through while it was still raining. I looked for a rainbow but couldn't find one in front of me.

I wasn't about to look behind me this close to Alaska.

Crossing Into Alaska

Stewart is a small town just across the border from Hyder, Alaska. When we pulled into town, I knew we were close.

I was excited.

We stopped and filled up our tanks so we won't have to worry about doing it tomorrow.

I was a little nervous I might get emotional when we crossed into Alaska. I silently wished I could cut off my headset so Mike wouldn't hear me, just in case I did.

Fifty-year-old men aren't supposed to get emotional. At least that's what my Dad taught me—and he was usually right.

It was still raining, but that didn't matter. We were one border crossing from being back in the United States, except this time we wouldn't be in the Lower Forty-Eight.

At exactly 5:30 p.m. we showed our passports one more time and rode across the border into Alaska.

We did it! We rode from Alabama to Alaska!

I was thrilled, exhausted—cold and wet.

Final Destination

Hyder is known as the "Friendliest Ghost Town in Alaska."

It has a certain charm of how things used to be.

As we pulled in, I couldn't help but wonder what it looked like when it was a booming mining town in the 1920s.

Originally, we planned on camping while we were here. That was before we rode all day in the rain.

We made a real-time decision to look for a hotel.

We had heard good things about the Sealaska Inn (a couple of miles across the border) and headed there.

The Sealaska is a window into the past. A handful of motorcycles were scattered around the parking lot when we arrived.

We weren't sure where to inquire about a room but saw a sign pointing to the bar on the ground level. We walked in and were greeted by several patrons in riding gear gathered around a table.

"You check in with the lady at the bar," a man said.

"Thanks."

We walked up to the bartender (hotel receptionist) and asked if there was room in the inn. I prayed she would say "yes."

"We have a deluxe room for $79 with two beds and a bath."

Her description and price sounded great. Neither of us needed anything elaborate. Hot water and heat would be nice. At this point, we would have been happy with an empty room with a spot for two sleeping bags.

Compared to camping, this place is the Ritz Carlton.

She handed us a key and told us to pay when we left.

She didn't swipe a credit card or ask us our names.

We walked up the stairs (attached to the outside of the hotel) to our room. The room is modest but plenty good enough.

"Mike, I would pay $200 for a hot shower."

Within the hour, I had one for half of 79 dollars.

First Meal in Alaska

Hyder's Glacier Inn Restaurant close by was our choice for dinner. We walked over and were immediately seated.

The restaurant was nice. I ordered seafood, and Mike ordered a sandwich. While we were waiting for our food, one of us was "Hyderized." This involved drinking a shot of 151 proof alcohol.

Another item checked off *my* bucket list.

The food was good—much better than either of us expected.

Final Thoughts

I'm in our hotel room, sitting up in bed, writing this ride report. I suppose a desk would have cost extra.

My friends say I'm somewhat of a coffee snob. I tell you this to highlight how good the latte at Bugwood Bean really was.

Even by Italian standards, it was outstanding.

Today, we made it to Alaska. Regardless of what happens from this point forward, we've accomplished what we set out to do.

I wish we could stay here longer, but we only have tomorrow. Commitments in our normal lives dictate that we head back.

The only stop we made on the way to Smithers was to take a picture of a billboard that read,

"Fort St. James … World Class Chicken Racing."

When I saw the sign, I wondered if I was seeing things.

Was the wet and cold cutting off blood flow to my head?

Could butt pain cause my brain to hallucinate?

Did I read the sign correctly?

I knew Mike wanted to make it to Alaska before dark—but several miles past the sign, I couldn't help myself.

"Mike, I'm going back to photograph that sign."

"Okay, I'll pull over and wait for you."

Places Traveled: British Columbia and Alaska
Miles Ridden: 437.1

Reflections One Year Later

DAVID'S THOUGHTS

We spent most of the day riding in yucky weather, and the miles clicked off too slowly.

When we crossed into Alaska, I was excited. I was proud of our determination to make it this far. I was thankful we were both safe. But I was also keenly aware of how hard the ride back home would be. I suppose ignorance is bliss.

Yes, I still had doubts about my body holding up.

Yes, I still worried about our safety.

But I couldn't wait to explore Alaska on our GSs.

This was a great moment in my life.

MIKE'S THOUGHTS

I found a navy blue rain jacket in Smithers. It was ugly, but it kept me dry. I rode with it on from Smithers all the way to Alaska. I don't think I got a drop of rain on me.

I didn't care about the fashion statement.

We had planned to camp while in Hyder, but the rain wasn't our friend—again. We voted unanimously to hotel-it.

A deluxe room offered two beds, a nightstand with desk light, and a bathroom for 79 dollars per night. It didn't have the luxuries of a TV, fridge, phone, overhead light, or fancy shampoos.

We didn't care.

It was dry and relatively warm.

Beginning of Ride Day Ten

Drying Gloves at McDonalds

Latte at Bugwood Bean—The Best I've Ever Had

Almost There

Closing in on Alaska

We Made It to Alaska!

We Sure Did!

Piece of Cake

The Sign Was Real

The Sealaska Inn

Third Leg

Hyder, Alaska

This leg of our journey was only a day and a half, but I remember every moment like it was yesterday.

Alaska was better than I imagined it would be.

Alaska

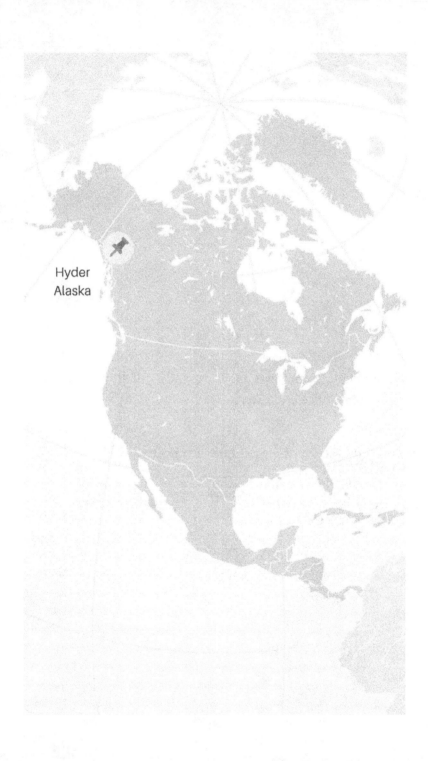

Hyder
Alaska

TWENTY-SIX

Ride Day Eleven

ALASKA

SATURDAY
HYDER, ALASKA

M ike and I got up early because we didn't want to waste a moment of our one day in Alaska.

We are about 70 miles from the Pacific Ocean along the Portland Canal, which separates Canada from the United States.

When I opened our deluxe room door, the morning sun glared into our eastern-facing room. Hyder looked different.

Hello, Alaska!

The Sealaska Inn doesn't serve breakfast, but that was okay. I still have a bag full of CLIF Bars I hauled from Alabama.

I'm not sure what I was thinking when I packed so many.

Did I wonder if there would be restaurants along the way? Did I want to ensure I could make it home on CLIF Bars alone if I ran out of money? Did I want to score a world record for most CLIF Bars consumed in a 21-day period?

I really have no idea.

Fish Creek

Our first stop for the day was to watch salmon spawn. We suited up and made the easy two-mile ride to Fish Creek. Five dollars bought us access to a wooden deck overlooking the creek.

Senior citizens surrounded us. I felt young.

Some carried expensive-looking cameras with ginormous telephoto lenses. Others used canes and walkers to manage their day. In that moment, I felt fortunate I had arrived on a motorcycle—all the way from Alabama.

I couldn't help but wonder if there was an ambulance service at Fish Creek. I'm pretty sure my CPR certification has lapsed.

Salmon were everywhere, and we watched them passionately swim upstream until I started losing interest. Mike wasn't close to being bored. He was enjoying all this almost as much as a good NASCAR race on Sunday afternoon.

And as always—he was a stranger magnet.

I think people could sense his excitement. That, and we were wearing hi-vis gear. We stood out in the crowd.

Bears sporadically visit Fish Creek for food, and the senior citizens were hunkered down for the long haul, hoping to see one.

And so was Mike.

Several brought coolers filled with drinks and a meal or two.

Excitement was in the air, but I wasn't feeling it. Sure, it was cool watching salmon swim upstream (for about 15 minutes), but I didn't want my main memory of Alaska to be this.

I'm not sure if Mike sensed my lack of excitement.

I did mention a time or two that our tickets were good for the entire day—just in case we wanted to do something else.

Thank goodness there wasn't a museum on-site.

What felt like a long time later, we rode back to the hotel to freshen up and get a few bursts of Wi-Fi.

Hair Dryer

My riding boots were still wet from yesterday.

Since our room didn't have a hairdryer, I asked the owner/bartender/receptionist if she had one I could use.

I'll never forget the look on her face as she burst out laughing. I wondered if she had misunderstood my question, but I quickly realized that she was laughing because I didn't have enough hair to warrant a hairdryer.

Don't women know men have feelings too?

I'll admit I'm thinning a bit on top (okay, a lot), but from her laugh, you'd think I was a standup comedian.

I wish I could get my wife to laugh that hard.

She retrieved a hairdryer from her room, and I used it to dry my boots. I got what I needed, and she had a good laugh.

I suppose it was a win-win.

Lunch

We ate lunch at the Seafood Express Bus a couple of blocks off the main road. It was well worth the effort to find it. A popular online motorcycle forum gave Mike the idea.

A sign out front read *The Original Food Truck*.

Diana and Jim Simpson own the place. Diana told us that Jim does the fishing, and she does the cooking.

"We've been serving out of this bus since 1998."

Mike and I ordered fish and chips (halibut) that Jim caught this morning.

I don't usually get passionate about describing food, but the fish and chips were incredible—the best I've ever had.

I enjoyed watching people walk up and contemplate whether to stop. Once we knew for ourselves, we told everyone it was great.

Shopping

After lunch, we headed back into town and walked around. At one of the shops, Mike started messing around with a musical instrument that sort of looked like a guitar.

He later told me it's called a dulcimer.

The owner took a special interest in Mike—after all, he is the stranger magnet—and insisted he try it. He did, and by the smile on his face, you'd think he was walking barefoot in a stream.

Today I learned that Mike has wanted to take dulcimer lessons for years. Why didn't I know this already?

I think the owner thought Mike was going to buy it.

She had no way of knowing the bags on his bike were full.

Mike was hooked, and I feared it might be more difficult to pry him away from this than it was the salmon. I purchased some fudge and walked outside to people-watch.

A few minutes later, Mike came out.

"Mike, you should buy the dulcimer and have her ship it."

He decided against it—possibly because this trip is costing us a whole lot more than we've told our wives.

Salmon Glacier

After we visited several more shops, we suited up for a ride to Salmon Glacier, the fifth largest glacier in North America.

According to locals, the road to the top was washed out more than normal. I was excited and a bit nervous.

Our GSs are made for this sort of stuff—but are we?

We headed out with plenty of gas (we filled up yesterday) and started the 20-mile ride to the top.

The views on the way up were incredible.

At each pull-off, we were rewarded with a new perspective that surprised me. Parts of the road were gone, but nothing was so bad we couldn't cross. I'm not so sure a touring motorcycle could have made it with the roads in this condition.

I enjoyed the relaxed pace of the ride.

Gray overcast skies cleared as we climbed higher, and the temp dropped mile after mile.

When we got to the top, the sky was a deep blue.

The glacier looked uncomfortably powerful.

Artists were there trying to capture the moment on canvas. Somehow I knew they wouldn't be able to.

We stayed for a while longer, then headed down the mountain in the same direction we had come, stopping several times along the way to absorb Mother Nature.

Now I know why the parts manager at the Chattanooga BMW dealership (where I bought my riding boots) insisted that we ride to Salmon Glacier while we were in Hyder.

More Salmon Watching

When we got back to town, we stopped by Fish Creek. Everything pretty much looked the same as when we left.

Salmon were still swimming incredibly hard, and according to several watchers, there hadn't been a single bear sighting all day.

The crowd had thinned.

We stayed a bit longer, then gave up again and headed back toward town. Bummer. Mike really wanted to see a bear.

Portland Canal

When we got back down to sea level, the clouds had broken, and the sun illuminated Hyder in a spectacular way. Everything looked different compared to yesterday, or even this morning.

We rode to the Portland Canal overlook and enjoyed the most picturesque time of the day—the afternoon sun. I said three words in my helmet to describe the moment.

"This is it."

Mike didn't respond.

We absorbed the beauty, took photos, then headed back to our hotel. There, we freshened up, then walked to dinner at the same place as last night. Why take a chance?

We enjoyed dinner without getting Hyderized, then walked back to the Sealaska Inn and called it a night.

Final Thoughts

When I left Alabama on this journey, I had few thoughts of what Alaska might be like. I had heard that it was beautiful, and the mosquitos were horrific.

The former turned out to be true, the latter not so much.

My mosquito net is still stuffed in my camping bag, and I've only used mosquito repellent on camping nights.

The Sealaska Inn promised high-speed internet, but it was far from high-speed and even farther from reliable. I found a spot by an electrical meter near the stairs that gave me occasional bursts of weak service.

I spent longer than I should have standing there.

I hope I don't grow an extra ear on the ride home.

I'm glad we didn't camp because the campground looked wet every time we rode by, and because bears are a real threat in these parts. Just so you know, Hyder is also known as the "Grizzly bear capital of southeast Alaska."

Our one day in Alaska was everything I'd hoped for and more. Salmon watching was entertaining, fish and chips were awesome, and Salmon Glacier was breathtakingly beautiful.

But the real treat for today was meeting the wonderful people in Alaska. I'll share their stories in the next chapter.

Places Traveled: Alaska
Miles Ridden: 48.1

Reflections One Year Later

DAVID'S THOUGHTS

Hyder is an anomaly. The only way in and out is through Canada. Hyder is in the southeastern tip of Alaska, and one reason why so many riders choose it as their Alaskan destination.

When we first arrived, I thought the town looked underserved and old. I was wrong. Hyder was much more than that.

The shops were quaint, and its people were warm. The restaurants served quality food. Salmon Glacier alone was worth the ride from Alabama. And being Hyderized was a blast, at least the parts I remember. I'm joking, kids!

When I first arrived at Fish Creek, I saw senior citizens struggling to get around. A few minutes later, I saw myself. The truth is they were doing exactly what I was doing—the best each of us could in that exact moment to live life to its fullest.

The pace of Hyder seemed relaxed. I wanted to stay longer.

Mike took several photos of me at Portland Canal.

He submitted one of them to *RoadRUNNER* magazine, which they published in their May/June 2016 issue.

I didn't buy any souvenirs while I was in Alaska. I've reached a point in my life where stuff burdens me. I secretly dream of living in a tiny house—or at least something much smaller than what I live in now. Sue isn't on board with my idea just yet.

If I had purchased something in Alaska, I would never be able to get rid of it. My kids wouldn't either.

This book is my souvenir.

MIKE'S THOUGHTS

Our afternoon in Hyder was breathtaking. David and I rode up to Salmon Glacier, one of the largest glaciers in North America.

It's a must-do if you're ever in Hyder.

Beginning of Ride Day Eleven

Mike at Fish Creek — Loving Every Minute

The Seafood Express — The Original Food Truck

Riding to Salmon Glacier

Salmon Glacier

Portland Canal — Published in
RoadRUNNER Magazine May 2016

TWENTY-SEVEN

The People in Alaska

A WONDERFUL SURPRISE

The greatest memories in Alaska came from the interesting people we met during our short stay.

Each person we spoke with had a unique story to tell—and for some reason, they were willing to share it with us.

I never envisioned this in all my planning.

Maybe it's because we were in a small town in Alaska far from home and wanted to connect with something familiar? Or maybe it's because we all discovered something about ourselves along the way and wanted to share it?

I wish I had this openness in my normal life.

Chris and Gary

We met Chris and Gary from Cumming, Georgia while we were watching salmon spawn at Fish Creek. They had been exploring Alaska for the past five months in their 32-foot motorhome.

Chris and Gary had a peace about them that was magnetic. Gary is a glider pilot instructor and has flown into Huntsville, our hometown, several times. Making a connection was easy.

We talked about traveling—and about exploring. It turns out that Gary knows someone Mike works with at NASA.

It's a small world.

Somehow the conversation turned toward home.

"We have a great chicken finger place near our home. If you're ever over that way, give us a call. We would love to meet you."

Gary gave us his email address and phone number. Mike and I agreed that it sounded like a great excuse for a ride.

Wes

We met Wes at the General Store. Wes is the General Store owner and mayor of Hyder. Wes is also a Vietnam veteran, former liquor store manager, and the self-appointed Sheriff of Hyder.

We learned all that in a matter of minutes.

"There's no law enforcement in Hyder," Wes explained.

"We take care of ourselves."

A .357 handgun lay on the counter for visitors to notice.

We talked about politics, race relations, and gun control. But these subjects seem too deep to include in a book about an adventure ride to Alaska.

So I won't.

Wes also told us that he liked living in Hyder because it gave him a lot of time to think. I wanted to hear more about what he meant but decided that some things are better left unspoken.

As we were leaving, Wes wished us safe travels and offered this:

"If your life isn't an adventure, you're not living."

Wow!

Greg and Ilene

We met Greg and Ilene at Portland Canal. Greg was the guy who pointed us to the bartender for a room when we checked in to the Sealaska Inn.

Greg and Ilene were on a 2006 BMW R1200RT (two-up) and had ridden from the BMW rally in Billings, like us. They had just come from Fish Creek and were excited.

I hated for Mike to hear the news.

"We just saw a bear at Fish Creek about 30 minutes ago."

Greg was reserved at first, but in a matter of minutes, he spoke to us like we'd known each other since grade school.

Several minutes later, he shared something deeply personal.

"I adopted my son 23 years ago when he was one month old."

Greg teared up as he continued.

"Last week, he thanked me for changing his life."

This was crazy—yet magical. Complete strangers were sharing something incredibly personal and heartfelt. I couldn't help but think of the people I work with every day and know little about.

When's the last time I've shared something personal with my best friends? When's the last time I've admitted I was scared about something—or happy, or sad?

Two people from North Dakota I had known for less than one hour showed me something I wanted to change in my life.

It was a pretty neat moment.

Another Dennis

The last person we met in Alaska was perhaps the most memorable of all. I first noticed Dennis's motorcycle, a 1995 BMW R100, in the parking lot at Fish Creek.

A custom paint job scribed a tribute to his son.

A plaque on Dennis's motorcycle read:

I would rather be ashes than dust!
I would rather that my spark should burn out in a
* brilliant blaze than it should be stifled by dry rot.*
I would rather be a superb meteor, every atom of me
* in magnificent glow, than a sleepy and permanent*
* planet.*
The function of man is to live, not exist.
I shall not waste my days trying to prolong them.
I shall use my time.

Dennis rode up as we were leaving. I felt an instant connection and desire to reach out. We rode over to where he pulled in.

I took off my helmet.

"I saw your motorcycle at Fish Creek," I said.

"I'm sorry about the loss of your son."

"Thanks. Samuel died five years ago in Afghanistan."

Mike and I listened intently as Dennis continued.

"Samuel's death changed everything. I asked my wife to come with me on this trip of discovery. She told me she didn't want to live with me anymore. I've been exploring Canada and the United States by myself for the past six months."

Dennis was mourning two losses.

He told us that he was on this journey to find healing and that meeting people was helping.

People approached Dennis even as we spoke.

"People are so good to me," Dennis said. "Total strangers leave cards on my motorcycle encouraging me and thanking me for my son's service. Some share stories of their own personal losses."

Talking to Dennis was a moving experience.

Mike and I were mostly silent as we processed it all.

Reflections One Year Later

DAVID'S THOUGHTS

Chatting with strangers isn't in my DNA—but for some reason, it was the norm for me on this trip.

The biggest memories of Alaska will always be entwined with the people we met and the stories they shared about life—and about death. The people in Alaska made a lasting impression on me, and I feel blessed to have seen into the hearts of strangers.

I'd call it one of the best days of a lifetime.

MIKE'S THOUGHTS

My favorite part of our time in Alaska was walking through town and meeting people.

Wes, the General Store owner, told us that Hyder almost had its own reality TV show. This doesn't surprise me. Caroline, from Boundary Gallery, insisted on giving me a dulcimer lesson. Diana, at the Seafood Express, served us fresh halibut out of a bus. Chris and Gary, from Georgia, invited us over for lunch.

These are the events that made our trip worth it.

Chris and Gary from Georgia

Hyder General Store

Wes Is the Owner of the General Store

Greg and Ilene from North Dakota

The Other Dennis

Caroline Giving Mike a Dulcimer Lesson

Fourth Leg

Hyder, Alaska to Colorado Springs, Colorado

This leg of our journey took us the long way toward home, and it was the most diverse. We saw snow-covered mountains, lakes and glaciers, lush greens, and desert browns. We saw bears, deer, sheep, chipmunks, and even a sign pointing to a Bigfoot crossing. We rode in near-freezing rain and dry desert heat. We rode on inter-states and backroads, through small towns and big cities.

We experienced victory and defeat.
And it all felt so incredibly real.

Alaska, British Columbia, Alberta, Montana,
Idaho, Utah, and Colorado

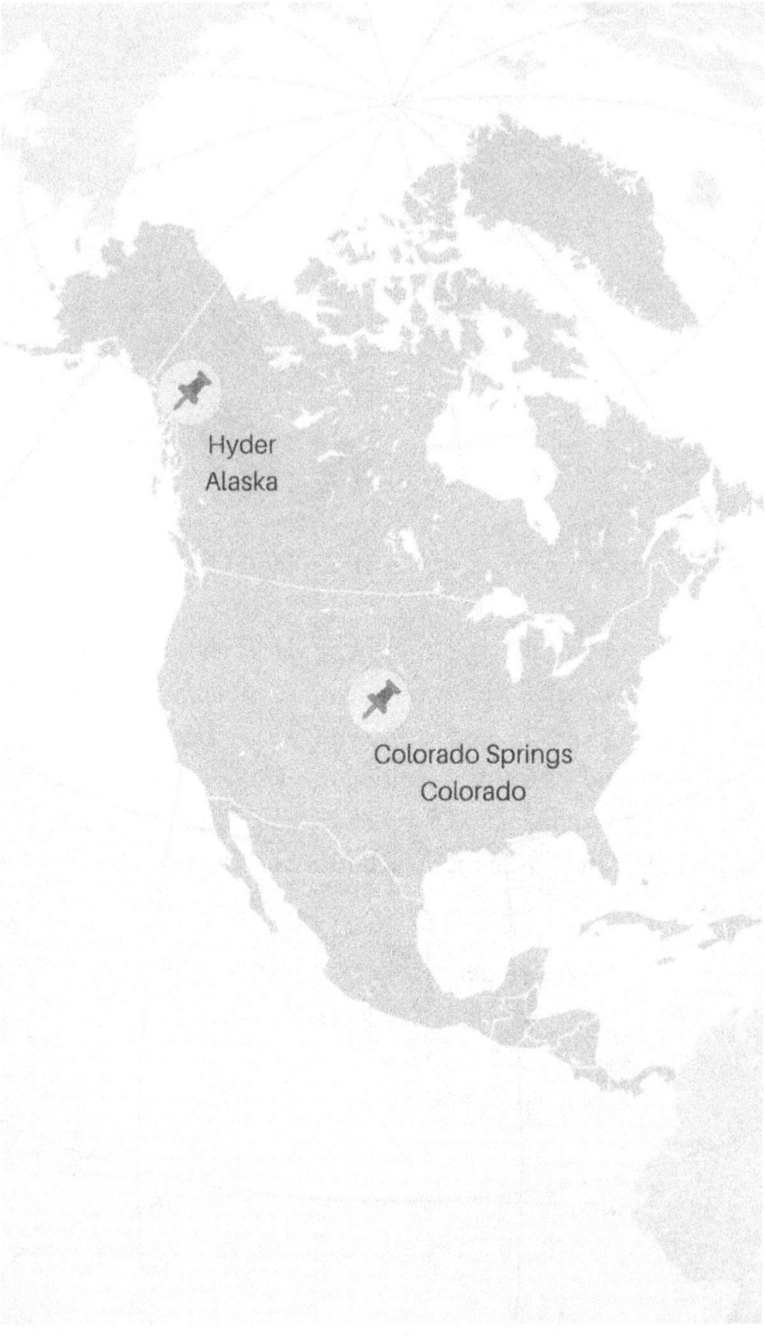
Hyder
Alaska
Colorado Springs
Colorado

TWENTY-EIGHT

Ride Day Twelve

WET AND COLD

Sunday
Hyder, Alaska to Prince George, BC

Today we left Alaska.

We didn't want to follow the same route back to the United States, but we both wanted to ride Going-to-the-Sun Road in Glacier National Park, and the roads in Canada are limited in that direction. We made a real-time change to the itinerary to backtrack through Canada using the same roads we came on.

When we loaded our bikes, it was raining. I felt blessed that it wasn't like this yesterday. We suited up with our full rain gear and headed toward the Canadian border a few miles away.

The border guards asked us several questions:

"Where are you going?" *Alabama in the States*

"How much money do you have?" *$200 each*

"Where do you work?" *NASA*

They scanned our passports and recommended several roads to explore on our way back. One guard said he thought space exploration was important. We acted interested.

We said goodbye, lowered our visors, and headed south toward Smithers. We had ridden this stretch of road once before and knew it was tedious, especially in the cold rain.

My GS said it was 48 degrees Fahrenheit. It felt colder than that. I didn't ask Mike what his said. I didn't really care.

My hands were the first body parts to get wet.

This wasn't the first time my "waterproof" gloves failed me on this trip. At one point, I thought about throwing them to the side of the road in disgust. But I didn't.

Canada takes littering seriously and punishes offenders with a $1000 fine. According to the road signs—at least.

For the first time on this trip, we were riding to a known destination. It felt comfortable but not quite as exciting.

Near Kitwanga, we turned left onto Highway 16 by the sign we stopped to photograph a couple of days ago.

I remembered how excited I was when I saw it the first time.

It didn't have the same magic this time through.

Smithers (again)

A little over 200 miles from breakfast, we arrived in Smithers, BC. I couldn't help but remember my dream latte from two days ago. I secretly hoped we could swing by Bugwood Bean for round two, but I knew that wouldn't fit into the timeline.

It was too wet and cold to enjoy sitting outside anyway.

We ate at the same McDonald's and ordered the same things we did the first time around. At least Mike has a better rain jacket. I told Mike I needed a few extra minutes to warm up and gather my thoughts. I was mentally exhausted.

"Take your time."

One hour later we geared up and continued on Highway 16 heading southeast.

Final Destination

We rode hard and made it to Prince George by mid-afternoon. We checked in to the Sandman, a modern-looking hotel we noticed on the way through before, and unloaded our gear.

After a few minutes of downtime, we walked to Mike's Steakhouse for dinner. It was just as good the second time around.

After a long meal, we walked back to the hotel to get ready for another long ride tomorrow.

Final Thoughts

Today was hard. I hated to leave Alaska. The weather was crappy. I struggled to stay focused and interested in what we were doing.

Places Traveled: Alaska and British Columbia
Miles Ridden: 431.6

Reflections One Year Later

DAVID'S THOUGHTS

We didn't talk much on the way to Smithers.

It was cold and wet. I was miserable.

All I could handle was putting one mile in front of the next. I clicked through the miles silently in my head like we did out loud on Ride Day Six.

The best part of the day was getting off my bike.

Mike's Thoughts

Leaving Hyder was depressing. We had reached our goal, and now we were heading back.

Home was a long way, and I think we both felt it.

Beginning of Ride Day Twelve

Gloomy Morning Departure from Alaska

TWENTY-NINE

Not Ready

FLASHBACK: *Ten days before departure ...*

I t's ten days before we're supposed to leave, and my life has been a whirlwind the last couple of months.

The overnight practice ride to test my gear hasn't happened—partly because I keep buying new stuff to replace my old stuff.

I just got back from a ten-day family vacation in Europe—the one my wife conjured up when I told her that I wanted to ride to Alaska—and work has been a nightmare.

I still don't have a tent, sleeping bag, or hi-vis helmet.

This isn't like me.

I can't stop buying stuff because I know I can get away with it. When Sue notices something new, I tell her it will make me safer.

Trust me. She's only noticed a fraction of what I've purchased.

Whoops. I guess I just blew that.

My To-Do List is still a mile long. If I had another month, I think I'd be more excited. Instead, I feel rushed.

Just between you and me, I'm not ready.

THIRTY

Ride Day Thirteen

BIGHORN SHEEP

MONDAY
PRINCE GEORGE, BC TO RADIUM HOT SPRINGS, BC

M ike and I agreed that the beds last night—two separate ones, just to be clear—were the most comfortable so far. *I don't suppose we can stay here another night?*

I knew the answer and didn't even joke with Mike.

Today we decided to backtrack on the same roads we rode on Ride Days Eight *and* Nine because those days were fairly short.

This buys us an extra day to take a longer route home.

Mike topped off his GS with oil (Mobil 1 Full Synthetic), and we loaded up. We pulled out of the parking lot and turned left onto Highway 16 heading southeast.

Jasper (again)

Some 230 miles later, we pulled into Jasper and found downtown.

We didn't see this part on our first pass through. By now, the sun had broken through the overcast morning.

We were dry, warm, and happy.

Parking lots were packed, and people were everywhere. Doesn't anyone work around here? We found a parking spot a fair distance from the shops. For the second time on this trip, I was nervous to leave my gear on my bike. I left it anyway.

We visited several stores, ate lunch, and found a gift shop that had Diet Mountain Dew.

Mike's a better friend when he has easy access to Diet Sun Drop or Diet Mountain Dew. For you non-Southerners, Diet Sun Drop is similar to Diet Mountain Dew.

It was a gorgeous day.

We shopped a while longer, then headed back to our bikes. I was nervous about what we might find when we got there.

Thankfully, everything was just as we'd left it.

We geared up, backtracked a few miles, and turned left onto the Icefields Parkway (Highway 93) heading southeast.

A short time later, I did math in my helmet and concluded we couldn't make it to Radium Hot Springs by sundown.

This meant we are about to violate a rule—again.

Wildlife Spotting

About 170 miles later (near Castle Junction), we turned right and continued on Highway 93 heading south.

A short time later, a bear crossed the highway in front of us. Mike was excited. We slowed to make sure she didn't have family following her.

She didn't, so we continued.

At least Mike got to see a bear, I thought.

The sun fell below the mountains to our west, and we reduced our speed. There weren't any cars around us that we could use to scare off wildlife. By now, it was almost completely dark.

Mike was leading when he called out.

"Deer on the left!"

I hit my brakes and saw the deer grazing five feet off the road. It looked up at me. I thought it was going to dart in front of me, but instead, it ran into the woods.

This moment could have been a real turning point on the trip and precisely the reason we made a rule not to ride at night.

We kept going because we didn't really have a choice. It started sprinkling when the road signs signaled we were about 40 miles from Radium Hot Springs.

We slowed our pace even more.

Final Destination

One hour later, we pulled into Radium Hot Springs.

For the first time on this trip, we arrived without a hotel reservation. We were keeping our options open for camping, but we both preferred a room with a real roof.

We were nervous but kind of excited too.

Riding into town without a room felt adventurous.

We filled our bikes with gas and stayed under the protection of the canopy overhead. Since Mike has made most of the reservations so far, I pulled out my phone and started searching.

The Bighorn Hotel had good reviews, so I hit the dial button.

"Yes, we have a room with two beds for $75."

"We will be there in three minutes."

My wife prefers hotels that accumulate Hilton Honor points, but the Bighorn Hotel was plenty good enough for two guys. The owner was friendly, and we parked our bikes next to our room.

We walked to dinner at a pizza joint close by. On our way, we saw bighorn sheep roaming around like they were pets.

Like you might imagine, they are sheep with, um, big horns.

They didn't seem concerned about us, so we weren't concerned about them—even though I couldn't help but wonder what it would look like if one of them rammed a human. Wow.

We took the pizza back to the hotel room and ate it there. We were hungry. It was good.

Final Thoughts

I'm sitting in our hotel room writing this ride report.

I looked forward to this ride today because some of the most breathtaking views on the way to Alaska were on this segment of the journey—including Bow Lake.

But today looked different.

It was overcast for the first half of the day, and everything was a shade of gray. The turquoise water in Bow Lake we saw five days ago looked bland in comparison.

It's like being disappointed with an average sunset because you saw a breathtaking one yesterday. Today made me appreciate what we saw on our first time through—even more.

And for that, I am thankful.

Places Traveled: British Columbia and Alberta
Miles Ridden: 459.0

Reflections One Year Later

We took too long in Jasper, which left us riding at night. We saw more wildlife than I originally admitted, including deer.

All this made me think of Larry Grodsky, well-known motorcycle instructor and author, who died in a motorcycle accident in

2006 when he hit a deer while riding at night. Larry was a good friend and colleague of one of my motorcycle mentors.

Tonight, we dodged a bullet we shouldn't have had to.

Beginning of Ride Day Thirteen

Mike Adding Oil in Prince George

Diet Mountain Dew Makes Life Good

Riding at Night Was Always a Mistake

One of Many Wildlife Signs Along the Way

THIRTY-ONE

Call From My Son

"DAD, SOMETHING'S WRONG WITH MY TRUCK."

Somewhere in Canada ...

Mike and I were stopped for gas when I heard my phone ringing inside my helmet.

I pulled it out of my pocket and saw that it was my son, Drew.

I only have a few rules in my life, and answering the phone (regardless of what I'm doing) when Drew calls is tops on the list.

If Drew calls, I pick up. Every-single-time.

My friends know this.

My work colleagues know this.

My family knows this.

This is a rule for a reason. If Drew needs money, he texts me. If he wants to talk, he usually calls Sue.

If he's in trouble or needs help, he usually *calls* me.

When I saw it was him, I yanked off my helmet and answered the phone directly so I could hear him more clearly.

"Hello."

I naively hoped he was calling to ask about my trip. But deep inside, I knew this probably wasn't the case.

"Dad. Something's wrong with my truck."

"Okay, son. Tell me what it's doing."

"Well, I was driving on Highway 72, and the engine died, so I pulled into the Smokeys BBQ parking lot."

I paused for a moment, realizing it could be worse.

"Okay, what did it do before it quit?"

"It made a loud bang. Oil is gushing out of the engine."

I may have been thousands of miles from home, but it didn't take me long to assess the severity of the situation.

"Son, that's bad. Call our repair shop and have it towed."

I was managing the situation surprisingly well until this.

"Dad, I'm on my way somewhere. Can you call them?"

"Well, son, I'm in the middle of Canada on my way somewhere too. You need to call them. I'll send their number."

"Okay, bye."

Reflections One Year Later

It turns out Drew did the impossible. The owner of the shop called me several days later with the news.

"David, it's bad. The engine is shot.

"I don't know what to tell you here. These 3.4-liter engines are bulletproof. This is only the second time I've seen one of them fail. A used engine from a wrecked truck will cost $4000."

European vacation, Alaskan adventure, 4Runner engine.

My life in 2015 was expensive.

THIRTY-TWO

Ride Day Fourteen

GLACIER NATIONAL PARK

TUESDAY
RADIUM HOT SPRINGS, BC TO CORAM, MONTANA

Today is my 25th wedding anniversary.

What kind of woman lets her husband ride a motorcycle to Alaska without her on their 25th anniversary?

A great one. She's a keeper!

Thanks, Honey—and Happy Anniversary.

Today was about crossing the border back into the U.S. and riding Going-to-the-Sun Road in Glacier National Park.

The Bighorn Hotel didn't serve breakfast, so we ate a CLIF Bar while we were loading up. A few minutes later, we pulled out and turned right onto Highway 95 heading south.

It was a great morning to be on a motorcycle.

Eighty miles from breakfast, we turned left onto Highway 93 near Cranbrook, BC. From that point, we were no longer backtracking on the same roads we used on the way *to* Alaska.

I couldn't tell the difference. The ride felt methodical.

My mind was fixated on being back in the States.

A little more than 160 miles from our last CLIF Bar, we pulled up to the border crossing at Rossville, Montana—60 miles west of where we crossed into Canada seven days ago.

This crossing felt different.

I was more than confident they would let us through.

We both have Alabama plates and talk with a Southern accent.

The border guard asked Mike a few questions, then signaled him through. I pulled up, took off my helmet, and presented my passport. I really needed an extra hand to do this gracefully.

A few questions later, the gentleman made my day.

"Welcome home, Mr. Mixson."

"Thank you," I said.

I started my GS and pulled up to where Mike was waiting. I got off my bike and took a photo of a sign.

"Welcome to the United States of America."

I felt a sense of relief we made it back to our native country.

The currency is familiar, speed limit signs show miles per hour, and friends without a passport can help us.

We put on our gear and continued on Highway 93 heading south. It's odd how the highway number stayed the same when we crossed into the United States, yet the road number changes when I cross from Alabama into Florida on the way to the beach.

I'm confused.

We rode for 110 miles into the United States, then turned left onto Highway 40 just past Whitefish, Montana.

A few miles later, we continued on Highway 2 heading east.

Glacier National Park

Today we approached Glacier National Park from the west. The wildfires are on the east side of the park, and by entering from the west, we hoped to be able to see more of the park.

We missed it on the way *to* Alaska because it was closed. Mike modified our route back to Alabama so we could ride it.

We stopped for a picture at a Glacier National Park sign, then rode Going-to-the-Sun Road up the mountain toward Logan Pass. Going-to-the-Sun Road is considered by many to be a top ten road for motorcyclists.

The ride was everything I had hoped for, complete with gobs of switchbacks and spectacular views of the mountains around us.

Logan Pass is located along the Continental Divide, and the Visitor Center is at the highest point. When we got to the top, we parked and started walking toward the Visitor Center.

A few seconds later, I looked back, and Mike was gone.

Like before, Mike had wandered off like a distracted child.

I scanned the area and spotted him talking to a park service shuttle driver. Mike wants to drive a bus at Disney World when he retires, so talking to bus drivers in tourist spots makes him happy.

Once Mike finished chatting with another stranger, we walked a few hundred yards to the Visitor Center.

It was packed.

We may have seen more people at Glacier National Park than we did in Canada the entire time we were there.

We walked around for an hour or so, enjoying the views and taking pictures, then headed back to our bikes and geared up.

Going-to-the-Sun Road was closed to the east, so we headed back down the same way we came up.

The ride down was just as pleasant.

The park campground doesn't take reservations. It operates on a first-come, first-served basis.

Find an empty spot, claim it, then pay for it.

We rode through the campground looking for an open spot but couldn't find one, so we stopped for a snack and to regroup. Mike remembered seeing a campground near Coram, Montana.

"That sounds fine to me," I said.

Mike called. They had openings. We headed that way.

Final Destination

Six miles later, we pulled into the Sundance Campground.

It is far from special, especially compared to the nice campsites in Glacier National Park we saw earlier.

We checked in, found our assigned tent camping spot several hundred feet away, and set up our tents.

For some reason, I was irritable, and I'm not sure why.

Maybe it was because I felt gross and didn't feel like camping, or because there wasn't a restaurant close by to eat, or because a family with noisy kids was tent camping next to us.

After we set up our tents, Mike built a fire (using my lighter), and we sat around looking at the radar, hoping it wouldn't rain.

If we were in a hotel, we wouldn't need to care, I thought.

A large group that looked to be several families was across the way. They were in three medium-sized campers, but sat outside around a large fire eating, laughing—and having a big time.

I was jealous. I wanted to sleep inside and eat what they were having. Instead, we boiled water and added it to food pouches.

Yummy.

About the time I started feeling sorry for myself, a gentleman from the group walked over and asked us if we wanted some apple cobbler he had just cooked in a dutch oven.

Like two men who hadn't eaten in days, we said, Sure!

We walked over and fixed a paper plate of cobbler.

I piled on as much as I could without being rude.

I wonder if our BMWs make people assume we're not thugs.

Final Thoughts

During dinner, Mike and I discussed options for getting home.

"We can go the most direct route," Mike explained, "or we can stick to my original route that takes us by some pretty cool places."

I knew Mike wanted to take the scenic route, and so did I.

"Let's take the long way home," I said.

We called it a night, and I retreated to my tent to write this ride report. It's nice to be back in the States.

Places Traveled: British Columbia and Montana
Miles Ridden: 296.4

Reflections One Year Later

Before you throw stones at me for missing my 25th anniversary, it's important to understand that Sue played a big part.

She wanted to do the vacation to Europe *before* my motorcycle trip, "Just in case I crashed." Remember?

The window for our ride was small to begin with. It's best to conquer Alaska on a motorcycle on the hottest days of the year.

Mike had constraints too.

His oldest son, Alex, was starting college at Auburn, and Mike wanted to be back to move him down.

Mike also had a family wedding to attend.

When I told Sue that doing Europe *before* Alaska would put me being gone on our anniversary, she didn't flinch.

"That's fine. I want to take the family vacation first."

And so it was. I traveled to Europe on a once-in-a-lifetime trip with my family. Then ten days later, I left for Alaska on a once-in-a-lifetime adventure with a friend. Poor me.

In hindsight, Mike and I should have secured a camping spot in Glacier National Park *before* we rode to Logan Pass. Mike came up with that idea a couple of months ago at lunch. A little late.

I'll admit it. I was grumpy at the Sundance Campground.

As I was throwing my tent up, I whispered to myself that I was tired of camping. I must have said it out loud because later that night, I overheard Mike telling Michelle.

"Dave's tired of camping. We're going to hotel-it from here."

Okay, I admit it. Mike's the camper on this team, and I'm the Hampton Inn guy.

That doesn't make me a bad person, does it?

Day 14
Is my 25th Anniversary!
Sue, you rock my world.
I LOVE YOU!

Happy 25th Anniversary

Posted In Ride Report for the Day

The Bighorn Hotel

Mike in Glacier National Park

Yummy Apple Cobbler

THIRTY-THREE

Canada

A WONDERFUL PLACE TO VISIT

B efore our trip, I didn't have many expectations of the ride through Canada. I simply viewed it as a necessary part of an overland trip to Alaska.

I was wrong.

The landscapes from western Canada to Alaska were spectacular—some of the best of the entire trip.

Canada felt comfortable—but different.

Most people we encountered were friendly and asked where we were headed. I suspect we weren't the first middle-aged men on motorcycles to answer, "Alaska." We saw a few Walmarts, an occasional McDonald's, and a mess of A&W restaurants.

Just an Expression

Canadians say "eh" a lot. The term seemed natural in no time, and I found myself using it, as a joke at first, then by habit. The expression is pretty versatile and can mean different things by its context. No worries, I'll bring you up to speed with what "eh" can mean.

Here are three examples.

EXAMPLE #1
Mike: What is the meaning of life?
David: Eh?
Meaning: "What?"

EXAMPLE #2
Mike: I'm a stud for starting a fire with flint, eh?
Meaning: "Right?"

EXAMPLE #3
David: I want to stay in a hotel tonight, eh?
Meaning: "What do you think?"

Where's the Gas?

Fuel stops were farther apart than I'm accustomed to, and motorcycles with small tanks would need to bring along extra containers. We never had a problem on our GSs.

How Fast is Too Fast?

Canadians drive on the same side of the road as we do, but they prefer kilometers per hour instead of miles per hour. No worries. Your motorcycle speedometer probably has a small kph readout.

If not, the conversion is pretty simple: 1 mph is about 1.6 kph. So, speed limit signs in kph will be higher than you're used to.

80 kph is about 50 mph.

50 kph is about 30 mph.

Final Thoughts

I underestimated how the ride through Canada would change me. I've never seen water a turquoise blue like we did at Bow Lake, or bighorn sheep roaming freely like we did in Radium Hot Springs, or mountains spanning for forever like we did in Jasper.

Canada, I underestimated you.

Sue is going to love Western Canada.

I can't wait to take you there, honey.

Wildlife Warning Sign

Somewhere in Canada

THIRTY-FOUR

Ride Day Fifteen

BLOWN AWAY IN IDAHO

WEDNESDAY
CORAM, MONTANA TO IDAHO FALLS, IDAHO

L ast night was the camping night from hell.
Babies in the tent next to us cried for most of the night.
I forgot how loud those little things can be. The tent must have
been full of them. *I'm thinking triplets, at least.*

Note to self: I really need to schedule THAT PROCEDURE
with my urologist when I get home.

If that wasn't bad enough, it rained for most of the night, and a
loud siren kept going off. It must have been right beside my tent.
When a siren goes off in Alabama, it means a tornado is on the
way. We run like hell to an interior room, put our head between
our legs, and ask the good Lord to forgive us of our sins.

Then I thought …
I wish I had pounded my tent stakes deeper into the ground.

Was this a tornado warning or something else? I thought about fleeing to the bathroom (the only structure with a real roof), but it had an offensive odor when I brushed my teeth before bed.

I had no idea what to do, so I did nothing.

I didn't check the weather because I didn't want to know. I just laid there wondering what it might feel like to be sucked up in a tornado.

I could see the headline ...

"Two men from Alabama were tent camping in Montana and IGNORED the TORNADO WARNING SIRENS. Their bodies were found in Idaho."

If that wasn't bad enough, a train track was 30 feet from my tent. I'm not sure how I missed this in the daylight. Trains announced their presence throughout the night by blasting their horns as they whizzed by. I could feel my tent being sucked in when they did.

Then I thought ...
I wish I had pounded my tent stakes deeper into the ground.

I'm not sure how many trains came screeching by during the night, but there were more than a few. On second thought, maybe I was hearing tornados passing overhead instead.

Either way, crying babies, tornados, and trains were all the fun. I imagine the campground owners got a sweet deal on this little piece of paradise.

Since neither of us was actually sleeping, Mike and I started packing at first light—mostly in silence. Our neighbors with the triplets from hell got up a few minutes later.

I half expected an apology, but they didn't offer one.

The dark side of me hoped I had snored all night.

Departure

We shook out our wet gear, loaded our bikes, and said goodbye to a glimpse of what the dark side might look like.

We turned right onto Highway 2 heading southwest.

Several turns later, we were heading south on Highway 83.

We didn't talk much in our helmets, and I enjoyed the silence. As the miles clicked through, I started noticing my surroundings and enjoying life again.

Riding a motorcycle in Montana will do that to a guy.

It felt like we were riding through normal places where people lived. Houses were on both sides of the road.

I imagined what people did for a living and for fun.

A short time later, I had a silent conversation with myself and decided that I was blessed to be in this exact moment.

I hope I didn't say anything inside my helmet.

If I did, Mike didn't respond.

Several miles later, we rode along Swan Lake in the spectacular morning light. It reminded me of Guntersville Lake back home.

When I packed up this morning, I thought we were heading back to the interstate. Instead, we saw a glimpse into normal life in this part of Montana.

Maybe Mike knew I needed "scenic" and changed the route. Either way, my soul appreciated smaller roads.

Ninety miles on my bike had erased last night.

We turned left onto Highway 200 at Clearwater, Montana and continued east. Several turns later (150 miles from breakfast), we turned left onto I-90 heading south.

Interstate at Last

It felt comfortable accelerating onto an interstate again.

My GS has plenty of moving juice even with my camping gear and CLIF Bars strapped on the back. Mike must have goosed it because I smelled oil burning more than normal.

It's been eight days since we've been on an interstate.

My mind and body were excited.

Call me weird.

For the most part, it was overcast. The sun poked through at points, and the contrast between the tan-colored wheat fields, blue skies, and gray mountains in the distance, looked magnificent.

Near Butte, Montana we merged onto I-15 heading south.

Uncultivated land in this part of the world is a light tan color sprinkled with some sort of field grass. Every now and then, we saw areas of green, which signaled man watered it.

In Alabama, Mother Nature provides plenty of water. Uncultivated land is filled with green vegetation.

I'm fascinated with trying to understand the irrigation systems around here. Some distribute water in a circle, like a gigantic lawn sprinkler—others water in a rectangular pattern.

Now I understand the different patterns of green I've seen in an airplane when I've flown overhead.

We clicked through the miles and continued south.

Rain

Weather experts didn't predict bad weather until later this afternoon, but they were wrong. We pulled over, put on our rain gear, and continued—breaking one of our rules in the process.

The light rain was no more than a nuisance. We stopped for gas and ate lunch at a McDonald's that was attached.

While we were eating, two men walked over and asked about our adventure. They had done something similar several years ago. They enjoyed telling us about it. We instantly felt a connection.

We chatted for a while longer, then geared up for the next leg. Mike checked his weather radar one more time.

"Dave, It looks like we're heading into bad weather."

We pulled out anyway and continued south on I-15.

Thunderstorm

I wasn't afraid of the bad weather. In my mind, we had seen it all. We had ridden in heavy rain in two countries and in more states than I cared to remember.

I figured storms in Idaho couldn't be any different.

I was wrong.

The sky to our south turned from gray to black. Mike looked at his weather radar and said these words in my helmet.

"Dave, it's about to get bad!"

A few miles later, a gentle rain turned to a full-up storm.

The wind started blowing in strong gusts from the west. I've ridden in strong winds before, and I know to stay relaxed and let the physics of countersteering keep me going straight.

But this was the worst I had ever ridden in.

By now, we were in the middle of a major storm. The crosswinds were relentless. Visibility was low. At times, our bikes were leaned over like we were turning. Instead, we were just doing what we needed to do to keep from blowing into the median.

We were in a difficult spot.

We looked for a place to pull off, but there weren't any exits. Why is it on this trip that we can never find a good spot to stop when we get into trouble?

The South isn't as rural as some are led to believe.

Stopping on the side of the interstate wasn't an option, either. Neither of us wanted to be a target for truckers.

I knew we were close to the limits of our tires and feared that one of us might lose traction with the next gust—especially since Mike's rear tire is nearly worn out.

I expected to lowside at any moment.

We kept going because we didn't have a better option.

Thirty minutes later, we spotted an exit in Dubois, Idaho and took it. We rolled up to a Phillips 66 feeling dejected.

I know we looked pitiful—again.

We loitered in the store for almost an hour and bought enough stuff to keep them from kicking us out. I'm afraid we made a wet mess. My mother wouldn't have approved.

While there, Mike called Michelle and asked her to book us a hotel in Idaho Falls, Idaho. We had planned on camping, but the thunderstorm changed our minds.

Michelle texted back a few minutes later with the details.

Once the storm passed, we geared up and continued south.

Final Destination

Fifty miles down I-15, we arrived at the Hampton Inn.

Mike asked the manager if we could leave our bikes under the massive covered check-in area. I tried to look dejected and battered when Mike asked her. Certainly, she could sense that we had just survived something horrific?

She paused for a moment, then said, "Sure."

It was all a put-on. I felt great—happy to be alive.

We unloaded our motorcycles, took showers, and walked to a Chili's a few hundred yards away. Mike took my request to stay within walking distance of a restaurant seriously.

So did Michelle. Thank you both.

Final Thoughts

Today we saw some neat parts of Montana and Idaho, survived a horrific storm, and both have laundry going.

The thought of having clean underwear makes me giddy.

What's not to love about life?

Mike is watching his favorite show, *Big Bang Theory*, and I'm in the lobby of a very nice hotel writing this ride report.

Honestly, I'm good for another night or two here.

Today was a good reminder that it's the thunderstorms in life that make the calm moments feel so much better.

I'm thankful to be alive. Thankful for this nice hotel. Thankful for two wonderful kids who don't cry during the night anymore.

I'm thankful to have an incredible woman to share the rest of my life with—even if she won't get on the back of a motorcycle.

I'm thankful to have a friend who's crazy enough to ride a motorcycle to Alaska with me.

Can you tell I feel better?

States Traveled: Montana and Idaho
Miles Ridden: 452.8

Reflections One Year Later

The evening at the Sundance Campground was a low point.

I was frustrated. I didn't want to be there. I needed rest.

One day later, life was great. I enjoyed riding on normal roads and seeing where locals live. I wondered what people did for work, what it might be like to live so close to Glacier National Park, and how my life might be different if I lived there.

I was amazed at the beauty around me.

I felt blessed.

Looking back at the photos, we crossed into Idaho without seeing the state sign welcoming us. I wonder if tight butt muscles decrease vision while riding in a massive thunderstorm?

Mike's first words after he took off his helmet in Dubois:

"Dave, I thought we were going to die."

"Me too."

Beginning of Ride Day Fifteen

Beautiful Morning in Montana

"Dave, It's About to Get Bad"

Bikes Parked Under Canopy at Hampton Inn

Hello Idaho

THIRTY-FIVE

More Mistakes

FLASHBACK: *Four days before departure …*

I t's four days before we're supposed to leave.
In addition to changing motorcycles, I just purchased new riding boots, a helmet, and a riding jacket—and there's no time to break them in or test them out before we leave.

This is so not like me.

You don't hike the Appalachian Trail with new boots or run a marathon with untested gear. Stiff riding boots and an uncomfortable helmet can be disastrous.

I wonder if I should take my old helmet, just in case.

But David, you don't have enough room.

I also did the unthinkable. I purchased the same motorcycle helmet Mike has. I tried to find something I liked better, but I couldn't. I selected the Shoei, mainly because it is hi-vis yellow and has an internal tinted sun visor that flips down inside the helmet.

With this model, I won't have to wear sunglasses, a huge plus —especially considering it gets hot and sticky inside a motorcycle helmet in the middle of summer.

I asked Mike if he was okay with me having the same helmet, and he said he didn't care. When you're over fifty, you don't have to worry so much about etiquette.

I purchased a hi-vis yellow riding jacket, different than Mike's, but just as visible. I became a fan when Mike got one years ago.

I was amazed at how much easier I could spot him.

Reflections One Year Later

New helmets have stiff pads. The cheek pads in my new Shoei were so tight that if I wanted to close my mouth without biting my cheeks, I had to close my lips and blow up my mouth, first.

Chewing gum was out of the question.

Talking on the headsets clearly enough was a challenge.

Truth be told, the only reason I changed helmets was that my old helmet (yellow but not hi-vis yellow) clashed with my new riding jacket. I can't say for sure, but I might have led my wife to believe otherwise.

I have fashion limits too.

THIRTY-SIX

Ride Day Sixteen

SPECTACULAR DESERT

THURSDAY
IDAHO FALLS, IDAHO TO GREEN RIVER, UTAH

The down comforters at the Hampton Inn were fabulous.
On top of that, I have clean clothes and can sit by total
strangers again without worrying about offending them.

We splurged and took our time at the free continental breakfast bar. I enjoyed drinking coffee and catching up on the national news without feeling rushed.

Life feels good.

Today was about getting closer to Colorado, and we had to go through Idaho and Utah to do that.

When we pulled out, it was an enjoyable 58 degrees according to my GS. Mike's said it was 59. We both added a liner to our riding jackets and selected winter riding gloves for the first part of our day. We left the Hampton Inn at 9 a.m. and headed south on I-15 toward Salt Lake City, Utah.

Everything looked different than it did yesterday.

Crops glowed in the morning sun.

There's something magical about a deep green field of Idaho potatoes planted next to a golden field of wheat.

I called an audible in my helmet for a photo stop.

The fence bordering the interstate was farther from the pavement than it was in South Dakota. Mike stayed on his motorcycle, and I hustled the 40 yards to the fence boundary for pictures—with my helmet still on. Someone on the team needed to make the sacrifice, and I was more than willing to do it.

As I was jogging through the thick brush, I wondered what type of snakes live in Idaho. That, and could their fangs penetrate my riding boots?

Luckily, I never learned the answer to either question.

When I got back to my bike, I secured my camera, put on my gloves, and told Mike I was ready.

We accelerated hard and merged back onto I-15.

About 120 miles from breakfast, we were at the Utah border. I called for another stop to photograph the state sign welcoming us. I moved quickly because I knew we were violating the same rule for a second time since sunup.

I could tell Mike wasn't thrilled about the stop. Two minutes later, we pulled back onto I-15 and continued south.

Lunch

Eighty miles into Utah (just north of Salt Lake City), we stopped for lunch at In-N-Out Burger. It was packed.

Mike had eaten at one before and insisted we try it.

While we were eating, Mike called several BMW motorcycle dealerships along our route to see if they had a rear tire in stock that would fit his bike.

Mike's rear tire had 3,000 miles on it when we left Alabama.

We knew it would need to be replaced somewhere.

Now was that somewhere.

Over the phone, Mike explained the situation and asked if they could replace the tire while we waited. The service manager at BMW Motorcycles of Salt Lake City was the most willing to help.

"Tell me when you'll be here, and I'll work you in."

Mike told him we would be there in less than an hour.

We finished eating and headed that way.

New Tire

Forty miles down I-15, we pulled into the dealership located just off the interstate. The service manager's name was Mike too.

He was waiting for us when we arrived.

"I'll put you at the front of the line and get you fixed up as quickly as possible."

I wondered if everyone in Salt Lake City was this nice?

He pointed us to the customer lounge and said he would call us over the intercom system when it was ready.

Mike (my friend) and I looked at new BMW motorcycles in the showroom, and one of us enjoyed a free cup of coffee.

"Mike, if I were rich, I'd leave with a new GS."

But I'm not rich—at least I don't think I am.

A little over an hour later, Mike (the service manager) made an announcement that Mike (my friend's) motorcycle was ready.

Mike walked back and settled up with a credit card.

Mike thanked Mike for helping us out, then we geared up and rode one block back to I-15 and continued south.

By now, traffic was horrible.

We zipped into the HOV lane, rode 30 miles to Provo, Utah, then turned left onto Highway 6 heading southeast.

Hot and Dry

Since Mike is the navigator, the next stretch of road—all the way to Green River, Utah—was a pleasant surprise for me.

The sky was blue, and except for the intense heat, it was a great day to ride a motorcycle. As we continued east, greens faded to tans and browns. As far as the eye could see, there was nothing but field grasses, rocks, and sand.

I'm not positive what the dictionary meaning of a desert is, but it sure seemed like we were smack-dab in the middle of one.

The heat was dry and noticeable.

This morning started at 58 degrees Fahrenheit. This afternoon our GSs agreed that it was 96. We were on the other extreme of cold and wet that we had encountered just days ago in Canada.

Sixty miles later, we pulled over at Castle Gate, a massive rock formation that pauses long enough for a road to run through it.

Like always, I rolled to a stop and put my feet down to steady the bike. When I did, my right foot slipped on loose gravel scattered on top of the asphalt. My GS started leaning to the right.

In an attempt to save it, I picked up my right foot and grabbed another spot. It was too late.

At this point, the best I could do was try to keep my leg from getting pinned underneath. Almost like it was in slow motion, I gently let my motorcycle fall to the ground. Mike was shocked.

"Dave, what are you doing?"

"It's not like I did it on purpose."

Mike set his bike on the side stand, careful not to make the same mistake I did, then stood there ready to help me lift mine.

I asked him to move back while I took a few photos.

He rolled his eyes.

I snapped a few pictures, and then we lifted her back to vertical. With all my gear (and CLIF Bars), it was a full two-man lift.

I'm sure everyone who drove by got a good laugh.

I let the GS rest for several minutes to make sure all the fluids drained back to the right spot. Then we continued south.

A short time later, the skies turned overcast and gloomy.

We spotted a deserted gas station and stopped to investigate. It was way too creepy to explore. This place would make the perfect horror movie set. We took a couple of photos and imagined what it must have been like in its glory days.

As we continued, I was mesmerized by our surroundings. This was different than anything I had seen before, but exactly what I had pictured a desert to be like all my life.

I wondered why nothing would grow in the soil, so I told Mike I wanted to stop and walk around.

I can't help that I have a curious mind.

We pulled over, and I walked out into the desert. Two steps in, and I already had my answer. I took off my gloves and picked up a handful of sand. It was like a fine powdery substance. Even if it did rain here, the soil wouldn't be able to hold enough moisture to grow Alabama-type vegetation.

As I was walking back to my bike, I imagined what it would feel like to be stranded here after dark. Wild animals would need to be pretty aggressive to survive here, I thought.

I said a quick prayer as I pushed the starter button on my GS. Thankfully, she fired right up.

Final Destination

Fifty miles later, we pulled in at the Holiday Inn Express in Green River, Utah. I'm pretty sure I understand why this community is named for the river that runs through it. For the first time in what seemed like a very long time, I saw the color green—and water.

It's an anomaly sitting in the middle of a brown desert.

The hotel isn't anything special, but water and air conditioning are all we need.

We walked half of a mile to a highly-rated local restaurant for dinner. We both ordered buffalo burgers, one of their specialties. We enjoyed the burgers and agreed they tasted like lean hamburger meat for the most part.

For dessert, I ordered a ginormous cinnamon roll.

According to the signs, the place is famous for them—and I don't have any plans of being back in the area anytime soon.

Obviously, I couldn't pass this up.

"Dave, are you going to eat that whole thing?"

"Oh yes. It won't even be a challenge."

Every single bite was amazing.

Back to Hotel

On the walk back to our hotel, Mike and I talked about what we would do differently if we had this adventure to do over again.

Mike said he thought our riding schedule was too aggressive.

I said my biggest mistake was that I didn't have a tank bag.

All in all, we didn't come up with any significant regrets.

We also talked about the journey coming to an end. It's been an incredible ride—something I'll never forget—and something I'll probably never have the opportunity to do again.

Final Thoughts

When I said the down comforters at the Hampton Inn were nice, I wasn't kidding. I feel refreshed. On top of that, I have more than enough clean underwear and socks to make it to Alabama.

For the first time on this journey, we're getting closer to home faster than I want to. It feels strange.

A stock GS Adventure is tall and heavy. A loaded one is even heavier. I'm guessing my loaded bike (not including me) is over 800 pounds.

Frankly, I'm surprised it took me so long to drop her.

In case you want to know—5,610 miles from home.

Dejected? Yes. Devastated? Absolutely not.

I just looked at my pictures from today, and I don't think they do it justice. I saw my life differently. Maybe it was because I could spin around 360 degrees and see nothing but blue skies and desert browns—all the way around me.

That's okay. I have it captured in my head.

Oh yeah. I almost forgot. The padded underwear I purchased in Billings is working great. For the first time in my life, I think I might understand how a woman feels.

It just feels, well, sorta weird down there.

States Traveled: Idaho and Utah
Miles Ridden: 391.9

Reflections One Year Later

DAVID'S THOUGHTS

This ride day was a huge surprise for me.

Before we left Alabama, I focused on the ride to Alaska and what Alaska might be like. I didn't think much about our ride to home, and I certainly didn't imagine our ride through Utah.

I was twenty-something the last time I was in Salt Lake City. Sue and I had gone skiing in nearby Park City with some friends.

We drove into Salt Lake City for a day because both of us were so banged up from skiing that we needed a break.

Salt Lake City seemed smaller this time through.

The detour to get a new tire for Mike was easier than I thought it would be. I bet we weren't the first riders to ask to be worked in for a new tire on a motorcycle adventure.

Mike at BMW Motorcycles of Salt Lake City took care of us. He deserves a huge shout-out.

I enjoyed the relaxed pace of this day—and the surprises. The plate-sized cinnamon roll was the cherry on top.

Mike's Thoughts

Lunch at In-N-Out Burger was fantastic. I wish we had them back home. Riding through Salt Lake City was the ultimate Urban ride. I'm thankful we weren't killed by all the interstate traffic.

Once we got out of Salt Lake City, we were greeted with the beautiful Utah desert and afternoon sun. We managed to stop and take several great photos on our way to Green River, Utah.

The highlight of the afternoon was David dropping his bike at one of our many photo stops.

I couldn't help but laugh.

Then I helped him pick it up.

Beginning of Ride Day Sixteen

Mike Helping Mike Get a New Rear Tire

And It Only Took Me 5610 Miles

Between Provo and Green River, Utah

Ginormous Cinnamon Roll

Hello Utah

THIRTY-SEVEN

Ride Reports

FLASHBACK: *Several weeks before departure …*

We're supposed to leave in a couple of weeks.
While Mike and I were eating lunch today, we talked about my plan to write ride reports at the end of each day and post them online for our friends and family to follow along.

"Mike, what happens if we get into trouble, or have close calls, or struggle? Sue and Michelle will read the ride reports. I don't want them worrying about us."

Mike paused for a moment and smiled.

"Dave, I've already taken care of that—
I told Michelle you tend to exaggerate."

THIRTY-EIGHT

Ride Day Seventeen

MILLION DOLLAR HIGHWAY

FRIDAY
GREEN RIVER, UTAH TO DURANGO, COLORADO

The Holiday Inn Express didn't have down comforters, but I made it through the night just fine.

We got up like normal and went through our morning routine of getting ready. I tried to like the breakfast buffet, but I couldn't.

No worries. I still have a bag full of CLIF Bars.

We loaded our bikes, geared up, and rolled out of the parking lot a little later than normal. We turned left onto I-70 heading east for a few miles, then right onto Highway 191 heading south.

The landscape was still desert-like and beautiful.

A few minutes later, Mike said, "We're about to ride by Arches National Park. Do you want to stop?" He hated to ask me because he knew I would want to stop. But he also knew there was no way to hide it because we were riding by the entrance.

"I think we should stop," I said. "We can go quickly."

Arches National Park

About an hour after we left Green River, Utah we arrived at Arches National Park. We pulled in and paid the entrance fee (an unfortunate part of the process), then stopped a few hundred yards later at the Visitor Center for information.

Yes, there was a tourist video. And yes, Mike watched it.

We asked a park ranger what we should do with our limited amount of time. He recommended a formation a few miles away. Great. We'll be out of here in 30 minutes.

We suited up and rode up the winding road to the spot the park ranger described. This ride alone was worth the stop. The sun was poking through the clouds, and the sky was a soft blue. I drifted back from Mike—no one was behind me—and rode up at a relaxed pace so I could absorb the unique landscape.

When we arrived at the spot, we got off our bikes and walked to the rock formation to embrace the full experience.

A few minutes later, we headed back to our motorcycles.

But, I knew this wasn't the end.

"Dave, I'm going to ride to the next stop."

For a moment, I forgot I was traveling with the guy who likes to read every plaque and watch every tourist video.

This wasn't going to be a 30 minute stop, I thought.

By now, the sky was overcast, and all the rock formations were starting to look the same.

"Mike, go ahead, I'm going to rest. Get me on the way down."

I moved my bike to the meet-up spot and looked for a place to relax. I longed for a tree, but there wasn't one—not even a shrub. We didn't have phone coverage, so we couldn't talk in our helmets.

Thirty minutes passed, and I was bored.

I saw a happy group walking toward a large—you guessed it— rock formation, so I decided to follow them and act amazed.

I walked for about five minutes, and the red rocks got bigger as I did. No surprises there. I turned around and headed back to my bike. When I got there, Mike wasn't there.

I started worrying that something might have happened.

Was he still alive? Did he need help?

Why was it taking him so long to look at more red rocks?

Then I had flashbacks of Wall Drug and Mount Rushmore and Mount Robson.

Mike pulled up an hour later. He seemed happy and described a red rock formation he had seen that sounded pretty much identical to the ones I had seen. I acted excited for him.

I put on my gear and followed him down to the park entrance.

Two hours after we entered, we exited the park and continued on Highway 191 heading southeast. Thirty miles later, we turned left onto Highway 46 heading east.

Hello Colorado

The road changed to Highway 90 when we crossed into Colorado. I called for a photo stop to take a picture of the sign welcoming us.

I'm still confused why road numbers change at state lines but stayed the same when we crossed into Canada.

About ten miles into Colorado, I noticed that something was different. Desert browns had been replaced with green foliage. The change wasn't exactly at the state line, but it was amazing how the landscape changed in such a short period.

We pulled over several times to absorb the bigness of the day and to take pictures. I said "wow" in my helmet—a lot.

Thirty miles into Colorado, we turned right in Naturita onto Highway 145 heading east. Forty miles after that, we turned left in Placerville onto Highway 62 heading northeast.

Million Dollar Highway

By now, clear blue skies had turned to rain. We pulled over at a gas station in Ridgway to put on rain gear and check the weather.

The next stretch of road along Highway 550 between Ouray and Silverton, Colorado is called the *Million Dollar Highway*. It's ranked as a top ten road for motorcyclists. Mike had been looking forward to riding it since we left Alabama.

It's also one of the most dangerous roads in the world!

While we were getting gas, the attendant told us a motorcyclist had died last week about a mile up the road.

"The rider lost control in a curve and skidded off the cliff."

I didn't say anything. Mike looked down at his phone.

"Dave, it looks like the weather is going to get worse."

"Alright. I'm ready."

As we were leaving, the attendant left us with this.

"Please be careful. People die on this road every week."

Her words caught me off guard. Neither of us responded.

We took a left out of the gas station parking lot and continued on Highway 550 heading south. At this point, I knew this ride wasn't going to be the moment we had hoped for.

I simply wanted to survive the first curve, then the next.

The weather conditions deteriorated as we climbed to 11,000 feet. And it got cold. I was afraid to look at my temperature gauge. Twenty-five miles later, we rode into Silverton, Colorado.

Halfway to Durango

By the time we arrived in Silverton, it was pouring. We stopped at a Conoco gas station for shelter and to give the storms a chance to pass. We walked inside dejected (again) and met another rider who was in the same predicament we were in.

We purchased enough items to warrant our visit, checked the weather for possible breaks, and looked at a map. The radar didn't look good, and the map suggested the roads to Durango were even curvier than the stretch we had just ridden.

Forty minutes later, we decided to continue anyway because we wanted daylight all the way to Durango.

Mike was silent.

I was apprehensive.

The last thing I wanted to do was crash.

I knew the next 40 miles would be challenging, even in perfect riding conditions. I took a deep breath, put on my helmet, and said a silent prayer that we would make it to Durango safely.

Deteriorating Weather

We turned right out of the Conoco and continued on Highway 550 heading south. I decided in my helmet (silently, I hope) that my only goal for the next 40 miles was NOT to crash. I promised myself that I would come back to absorb this sliver of nature another day. Over and over, I repeated this in my helmet.

"Focus on good mechanics."

"Don't worry about the view."

"PEOPLE DIE ON THIS ROAD EVERY WEEK."

I wish I could have snapped my fingers and been in Durango, but I couldn't. I kept hearing the gas station attendant's warnings.

I don't think Mike was as concerned about the danger. He was more upset that we were riding a top ten road in crappy weather.

"Mike, let's take it easy."

"I agree."

Final Destination

We rolled into Durango, Colorado with a few minutes of daylight left to spare. I was mentally and physically exhausted.

But we were safe—and that was good enough.

For the second time on this trip, we arrived without a reservation. Just like in Radium Hot Springs, we pulled into a gas station and sought shelter. By now, it was raining hard.

We topped off our tanks since we were taking up space.

We both needed someone to help us find a room, but we only had each other. We pulled out our phones and looked for options. We called several hotels we had seen on the way in that looked decent. Hotel after hotel said they were full.

Great. What are we going to do if we can't find a place?

The last hotel on my list (sorted by positive reviews) was the Super 8. I called, and the man who answered didn't laugh when I asked if he had a room with two beds for the evening.

"I'll take it."

According to my map, the Super 8 was a couple of miles away. I could tell Mike was exhausted. He had led all day, and it takes a lot more energy to navigate in inclement weather.

"Dave, can you take the lead."

"Sure, it looks like it's about four miles from here."

We put on our helmets, pulled out into the rain, and turned right heading south. A few miles later, we came to a tee where we had to choose left or right. I didn't recall a turn when I looked at the map. I guessed "right."

About a mile later, I realized I wasn't sure if this was correct. I saw a nice Holiday Inn Express on our left and told Mike I was going to pull in and regroup. It was still pouring.

We walked inside looking pitiful (again). The hotel was nice, and I felt bad that we were getting their floors wet.

I could picture with near certainty that this place had down comforters like the Hampton Inn in Idaho Falls.

I put my "dejected" face on and walked up to the attendant.

"Do you, by chance, have a room with two beds for tonight?"

From the look on her face, she wanted to say "yes."

"I'm sorry. There's a conference in town, and we're full."

"Thanks anyway."

We walked to a carpeted area so we wouldn't make a slippery mess for paying guests and checked directions to the Super 8.

"Okay, Mike, I know where it is. Just follow me."

We put on our wet helmets, mounted our wet GSs, and turned south on Highway 60. Two miles later, we were there.

The Super 8 looked just like I had imagined from reading the reviews. We pulled under a small canopy with several other motor-cyclists who looked weathered like us.

I was exhausted—but happy.

We survived the day, and I was headed to heat and hot water.

We unloaded our stuff and ordered pizza.

Simple things go unnoticed until you don't have them.

Final Thoughts

Like a crash victim doesn't remember his crash, I don't remember anything about the Million Dollar Highway. In fact, I can't recall a single image of Mother Nature from Ridgway to Durango.

I was only focused on making the next curve.

Today wasn't what we had dreamed it would be, but it was far from a bust. I'm not working, or mowing the grass, or fixing the spot on my kitchen ceiling that's been on my list for way too long.

We're blessed that we made it without crashing,

Blessed to be doing something few get to do.

Blessed we have a warm place to sleep tonight.

States Traveled: Utah and Colorado
Miles Ridden: 301.1

Reflections One Year Later

DAVID'S THOUGHTS

I was upset we didn't get to ride the Million Dollar Highway on a clear day, but for Mike, it had to be worse. When you spend hours planning the route (like Mike did), you're more invested—and more disappointed when things don't go as planned.

I'm glad I didn't know how far out of the way we rode to see something spectacular that turned out not to be.

Mike carried that burden—without a single complaint.

One of my favorite pictures of the trip is of Mike in Durango when we pulled under the canopy at the Super 8.

His expression describes the day perfectly.

MIKE'S THOUGHTS

Riding the Million Dollar Highway was important to me. It's consistently rated as a top ten road for motorcyclists. I planned the entire route back to be far enough south so we could ride it.

I mostly saw the double yellow line—a huge disappointment.

We would have been better served with pontoons instead of motorcycle tires.

Arches National Park

More Rocks in Arches National Park

Hello Colorado

Colorado Curves in Good Weather

Million Dollar Highway in Bad Weather

Mike in Durango — This Says It All

THIRTY-NINE

Is This Real?

FLASHBACK: *One day before departure ...*

The final pieces of my camping gear are here.
Motorcycle purchased ... *check.*
Riding gear and helmet ready ... *check.*
Passport, cash, phone ... *check.*
What started as "We should ride our motorcycles to Alaska" has turned into a journey that few will ever attempt.

I have no idea what lies ahead, but I can't wait to find out.

The part I look forward to most is the unknown, the unexpected, the bits I can't envision even when I try.

How will it feel to ride a motorcycle for three weeks?

How will my mind and body react?

How will we handle unexpected problems or illnesses?

I don't expect—or want—everything to go perfectly. I want to learn something along the way: about life, about friendship, about overcoming adversity.

Adventure, teach me.

FORTY

Ride Day Eighteen

PIKES PEAK

T oday was about taking scenic roads to Pikes Peak.

We completed the typical morning routine and grabbed an individually wrapped danish at the breakfast buffet—if you can call it that—then loaded our bikes. We said goodbye to the Super 8 and took a right onto Highway 160 heading east.

Durango is a hotspot for off-roading. On our way out of town, we saw tons of signs offering off-road rentals and tours.

I'd love to go back and explore the area with my family.

Colorado Backroads

Once we made it out of town, I was mesmerized by the landscape. Riding in bad weather yesterday made me appreciate this morning even more.

Seventy miles from Durango, we stopped at an overlook near Treasure Mountain. The view was more than worth the stop.

Hundreds of chipmunks scurried around—happy as could be. We met an older man with his grandson and exchanged stories. I can still picture the excitement on the little boy's face.

They were both enjoying the day as much as we were.

A few minutes later, we put our gear back on and continued on Highway 160 heading northeast. Forty miles farther, we turned left onto Highway 285 heading north.

The next stretch was an anomaly. For the first time in a long time, the road was flat—and straight. Mountains poked up at a distance, and working farms surrounded us.

The views were simply incredible. I began to wonder if people who live here even noticed? This made me think of things I take for granted back home.

Do I take the time to enjoy Guntersville Lake?

Do I notice the different shades of green in spring?

Do I pause when I see a sunrise on the way to work?

Not as often as I should.

Lunch

We stopped in Buena Vista for lunch at K's Old Fashioned Burgers, a popular burger and ice cream joint.

Mike's daughter, Anna, ate there while she was on a youth trip several years back and raved about it. Mike thought it would be neat to eat there and send her a picture.

We ordered as takeout and walked to a park around back. I enjoyed watching people and imagining what their lives were like.

It was a great day to be on a picnic.

A young couple with a severely handicapped child ate near us. They looked happy and appeared to be making the best of what life had dealt them. I was moved. I longed for more information about their situation but didn't dare to ask.

In the moment, I felt too lucky.

This family doesn't have the same options that I do. I'm on a motorcycle adventure to Alaska with no real purpose.

It made me think of the blessings in my life.

It made me want to laugh more—and cry more.

I laid back on the picnic table bench and closed my eyes. I felt the sun adding warmth to my body and energy to my soul—and I longed for more minutes to enjoy the moment.

Onward

A short time later, we geared up, rode a couple of miles back to Highway 285, and continued north. Fifteen miles later, we turned right on Highway 24 heading northeast.

Clouds rolled in as we proceeded.

Mike checked the weather.

"Dave, there's a storm developing ahead."

We were both disappointed. What's the point of riding to the top of a very tall mountain when you can't see anything?

Pikes Peak was easy enough to spot from a distance. It's the highest summit of the southern Front Range of the Rocky Mountains in North America. As we continued, dark clouds formed in the exact direction we were heading.

By now, Mike was upset.

Riding to Pikes Peak was one of the things he looked forward to the most on this leg of the adventure. I'm pretty sure that riding the Million Dollar Highway and Pikes Peak required us to ride a long way out of our way to get home.

I heard Mike mumbling something about it in my helmet.

Mike checked the radar one more time.

"Dave, a storm is parked on top of Pikes Peak."

We stopped for fuel near the road that leads to the entrance.

Mike suggested as an option that we could bypass Pikes Peak and head straight to our hotel for an early evening.

"I'll do whatever you want, but I'm fine to give it a shot."

"Okay," Mike said. "We need to turn left."

Pikes Peak

We exited the gas station and backtracked one mile, then turned left onto Pikes Peak Highway. It was dry but overcast. A short ride later, we pulled up and paid another entrance fee.

Life isn't cheap.

I really should have brought more cash so my wife won't know how much this trip cost. I'm afraid I've left an electronic trail that might bite me in the backside someday.

Sloppy isn't usually like me.

The sky looked gloomy, but we proceeded anyway.

Mike took off at Mach speeds, and I proceeded up the mountain at a more relaxed pace. For some reason, Mike seems to prefer going faster on curvy roads than he does on straight.

We're opposites on that—and we're not even married.

The road went back and forth as we climbed. The switchbacks reminded me of Beartooth Highway. Sixty seconds after Mike left me, my headset beeped to signal we had lost communications with each other.

I didn't mind. For the first time in days, I could talk in private.

The overcast clouds broke just long enough for the sun to poke through. I hated to get my hopes up, but I knew Mike wanted to see Pikes Peak at its best—and so did I.

The temperature dropped as we continued to climb, and the views back down the mountain got better and better. I wanted to pull off, but I didn't want Mike to worry I had crashed.

As I continued, I saw Mike standing next to his bike, pointing his camera at me. I pulled in behind him and took off my helmet. Without saying a word, we looked at each other and smiled.

The views were incredible—and we still had higher to go.

My GS never skipped a beat.

When we arrived at the top, the parking area was packed. We found a space too small for a tiny car and parked both bikes in it. It was 82 degrees Fahrenheit when we paid our entrance fee. Now, our GSs signaled it was 48 degrees.

I could feel the difference.

We walked to the Pikes Peak sign and asked someone to take our picture. Then, we walked to the ledge on the north side.

It felt like I was in an airplane made of glass looking down. We towered over the other mountains to our west that we had ridden through earlier in the day.

This was better than I had imagined.

A few minutes later, we decided to split up.

Mike headed to the gift shop. If there's a museum in there, this might take a while. And I walked around in awe.

While I was walking around, several people asked me in disbelief, "Did you ride a motorcycle up here?"

I smiled and answered, "yes."

Trouble

An hour after we arrived, I started feeling lightheaded. Pikes Peak is 14,110 feet above sea level. The place I do most of my breathing (Huntsville) is 620 feet above sea level.

I knew this signaled trouble and that I needed to get down to a lower altitude where there was more oxygen.

All of a sudden, I felt overwhelmed.

How was I going to get my bike down the mountain?

How was I going to get *myself* down the mountain?

I was in trouble, and I needed to act quickly.

I found Mike and told him I felt lightheaded and that I was going to head back down before it was too late. I faked calm.

"Why don't you stay here?" I said. "I'll be fine by myself."

"No. I'll head back down with you."

I didn't have the energy to argue.

"Okay."

We found our bikes, suited up, and cautiously proceeded out of the parking lot. The first few miles were difficult for me, but I knew I didn't have to make it much farther.

A few thousand feet down, I felt much clearer.

Oxygen is good—all the time.

By the time we were back down to normal Colorado altitudes, the clouds had cleared to reveal a deep blue sky. We pulled over to photograph a road sign.

"Big Foot Xing. Due to sightings of a creature resembling Big Foot, this sign has been posted for your safety."

Final Destination

At the bottom of the mountain, we turned right onto Highway 24 heading east. Ten miles later, we took a left on I-25 heading north and rode another ten miles to our home for the evening, the Fairfield Inn in Colorado Springs, Colorado.

The hotel is nice.

Several restaurants are within walking distance—just like I like it. For one of the last times on this trip, we hauled in our gear, cleaned up, and walked to dinner.

Final Thoughts

I'm in our hotel room writing this ride report. Today was our last day on backroads. Tomorrow we take interstates to home.

Mike says tomorrow is another long day. My butt hurts just thinking about it. I wonder if I'll have long-term side effects in the buttocks area from this trip?

We're still 1,250 miles from home, but it feels like we're close.

States Traveled: Colorado
Miles Ridden: 366.9

Reflections One Year Later

The ride from Durango east to Colorado Springs was magnificent. I enjoyed seeing working farms with mountains as the backdrop.

People who see this every day are lucky.

I never told Mike this, but I was glad he left Pikes Peak when I did. My mind was in a fog. I knew I just had to follow him down for a few miles, and I'd be fine.

And that's what I did—slow and easy.

I still have no idea how far out of our way we rode to swing by Pikes Peak. Whatever it was, it was worth it.

Overlook Near Treasure Mountain

A Beautiful Colorado Morning

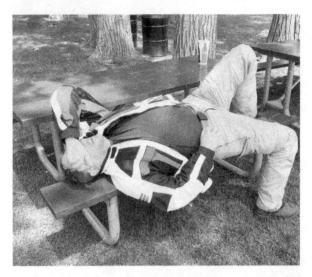

Quick Break After Lunch

Switchbacks to Pikes Peak

Pikes Peak Summit

Bigfoot Crossing Sign

Fifth Leg

Colorado Springs, Colorado to Home

This leg of our journey was about getting home—with a slight detour to ride one last top ten motorcycle road.

Interstates, heat, a close-call, and the emotions of this journey coming to an end.

Colorado, Kansas, Oklahoma, Arkansas, Tennessee, Mississippi, and Alabama

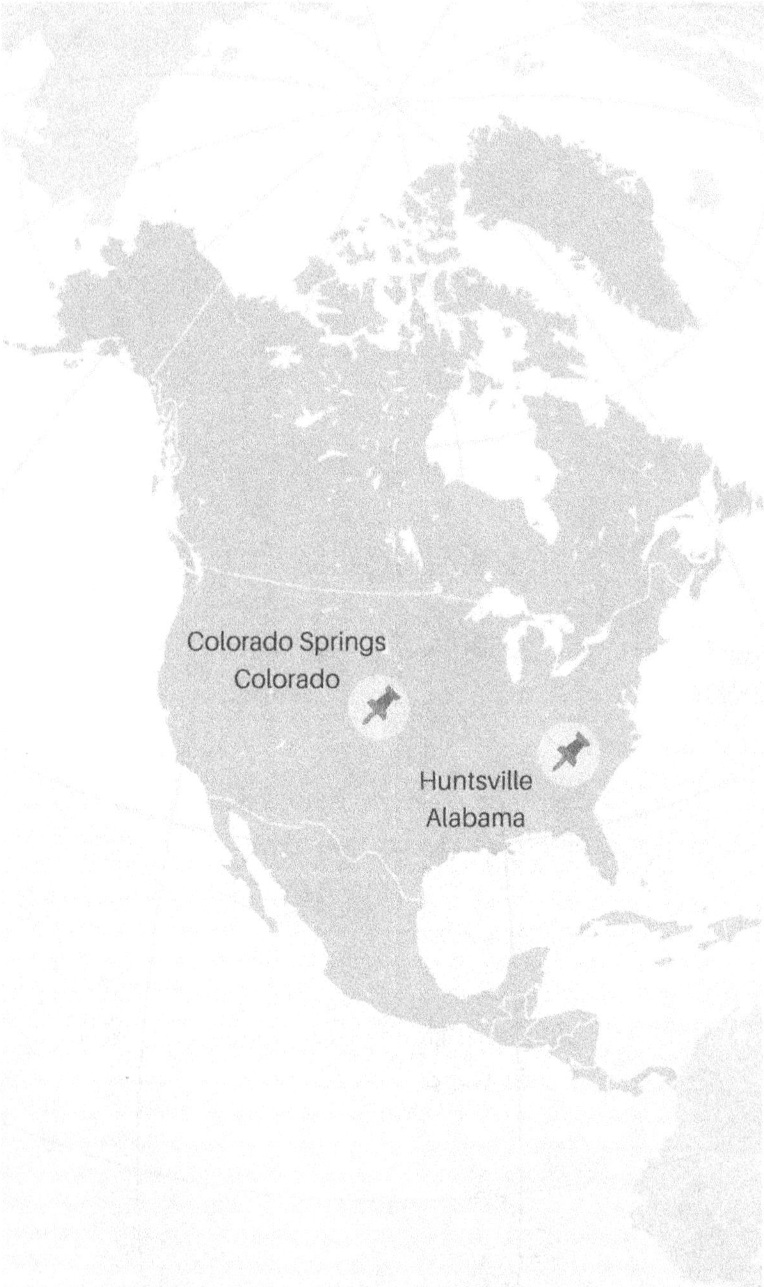
Colorado Springs
Colorado
Huntsville
Alabama

FORTY-ONE

Ride Day Nineteen

EMBASSY SUITES

SUNDAY

COLORADO SPRINGS, COLORADO TO TULSA, OKLAHOMA

Today was about getting closer to home. I knew we had over 600 miles to ride, but Mike wouldn't say by how much.

We followed our morning routine and pulled out at 8 a.m. A few hundred yards later, we turned left onto I-25 heading north.

Colorado Springs seems like a nice place to live.

Ten miles later, we exited onto Highway 24 heading east.

I enjoyed the open views on this clear morning. Mike made the comment that eastern Colorado looked different than western Colorado did yesterday. I agreed.

Fifty miles later, we turned right onto I-70 heading east. When we got up to speed, I said, "Let's go."

I'm certain Mike rolled his eyes inside his helmet.

It doesn't take a rocket scientist to understand that it's quicker to click through 600 miles when you're going faster.

I had already run the numbers in my head. A consistent seven mph faster would shave almost an hour off our ride time.

"Why don't you take the lead?" Mike said.

Without saying a word, I passed Mike and rolled the throttle back a little farther than normal—and held it there.

We stopped for gas once and were at the end of Colorado in no time. I called for a photo stop to capture the Kansas state sign that welcomed us (rule broken), then we pressed on.

Lunch

We rode for another 180 miles and stopped in Hays, Kansas for lunch. Neither of us had eaten at Freddy's Steakburgers, so it was the obvious choice for a quick stop.

It was delicious.

We geared back up, refueled a second time since breakfast, and turned left back onto I-70 heading east. We were now one-third of the way across Kansas and over halfway to our final destination.

But the last half of each ride day is always harder.

A tad over 100 miles later, we veered right onto I-35 heading south. We clicked through another 100 miles to Wichita, Kansas and continued on I-135 heading south.

We pushed hard with purpose.

By now, I was tired and don't recall much about our surroundings. My mind was focused on keeping our speed up so we could make it to the hotel at a reasonable hour.

For all I knew, we had way more than 600 miles to ride, and Mike was lowballing the number to make me feel better.

Oklahoma

Fifty miles later, we crossed into Oklahoma. I called for a quickie stop (rule broken) to photograph the state sign and to snap a few pictures of my motorcycle against the overcast sky.

A picture always looks better with a motorcycle in it.

The afternoon sun was intense. My GS said it was 102 degrees Fahrenheit. The high humidity made it feel more uncomfortable than the dry heat in Utah. It was all-out southern hot—something I understand perfectly but hate with a passion in riding gear.

Fifty miles past that, we exited onto Highway 412 heading east toward Tulsa. We stopped twice to pay for using the same road—two dollars, then one dollar a few miles later.

Paying a toll on a motorcycle isn't easy: motorcycle to neutral, helmet visor up, gloves off, wallet out, money to operator, wait for green light to proceed, wallet secured, gloves on, clutch in, visor down, bike in first gear, pull away without stalling. This procedure is even harder to execute when cars are stacked behind you.

I would have happily paid three dollars at the first booth.

I knew today's ride would likely push into dark. A short time later, the sun dropped below the horizon (rule broken).

My odometer clicked past 600.

"Mike, how much farther?"

Silence.

During the next stretch, Mike and I didn't talk much. My mind was fatigued, and my backside was killing me.

I should have purchased a better seat.

I wanted this ride day to be over.

Final Destination

We arrived at the Embassy Suites in Tulsa, Oklahoma at 8:44 p.m. I was giddy like a kid at the beach that I didn't have to set up my tent and sleep outside in this heat.

I felt like I'd just completed a half marathon and was about to enjoy pizza at the finish line. If you've ever run a long race, you know what I'm talking about.

I was so happy that I took a few selfies with an Embassy Suites sign in the background. I'm not sure that was very mature.

Embassy Suites

The Embassy Suites is exactly what I had imagined in my mind all day. The atrium area feels like a refuge.

We paid twice as much for the Super 8 in Durango. Painful.

We checked into our room and smiled. I'm glad we didn't stay at an Embassy Suites early in the trip because all the other hotels would have seemed dull by comparison.

Neither of us was very hungry, so we ordered an appetizer in the hotel restaurant and sat in the atrium and talked. I enjoyed a local craft beer, and Mike ordered a Diet Coke.

I wish I could have paused time.

Final Thoughts

I'm writing this ride report in a very nice hotel that Mike got for $100. He made a video exclaiming his prize and posted it online.

Maybe the Wood Badge guy on the team is really an Embassy Suites guy—just like me.

He'll never admit it, though.

It's amazing that neither of us seems to be tired of each other.

We talked in the atrium like we hadn't spoken in weeks.

That's pretty amazing when you think about it.

This adventure would certainly feel different if we got on each other's nerves. Really different.

States Traveled: Colorado, Kansas, and Oklahoma
Miles Ridden: 678.4

Reflections One Year Later

DAVID'S THOUGHTS

I'm starting to realize how often we ate burgers. It wasn't bad enough to kill us—since we're both still alive one year later.

But in retrospect, it probably wasn't the best choice.

Unfortunately, easy, quick, inexpensive food is usually fatty, highly processed, and slammed with carbohydrates. Not good.

This was our second-longest ride day of the trip. It was hot, but the heat felt manageable compared to Canadian cold and wet.

Maybe I like riding in the heat more than I thought.

When we pulled into the Embassy Suites, I was smiling as far as my lips would move. I prefer to stay in dumpy hotels on high mileage days and nice hotels on low mileage days.

I learned that on this trip.

Unfortunately, things like that don't always work out in the real world of adventure riding.

MIKE'S THOUGHTS

Kansas was big, flat, and boring. Riding in the heat was tough. Scoring the Embassy Suites for $100 was sweet. So much so that I made a video and posted it online to show my prize.

Hello Kansas

Hello Oklahoma

I Hate You

A Picture Always Looks Better
With a Motorcycle in It

Happy Happy Happy!

FORTY-TWO

Overcome With Fear

FLASHBACK: *One month before departure ...*

I wrote the following entry in my journal one month before we left on our adventure. I've never told anybody, until now.

I have serious doubts about riding a motorcycle to Alaska.

I haven't told anyone because I'm embarrassed.

I'm not worried about riding in inclement weather or breaking down. I'm not nervous about being away from my family or work. But I'm still apprehensive.

As odd as this might sound, I'm not worried about my safety either. I'm a grown man now, and I've decided to do this.

I can live with the consequences if something goes wrong.

Sure, I think about how a crash would affect my wife and kids, but I'm reasonably confident I can avoid dying, or I wouldn't go.

Am I being selfish?

The thing I fear most—to the point of wondering if I should call this trip off—is that Mike will be in a bad accident.

What would it be like to call Michelle and tell her?

What would I say to his family?

How would I handle losing another best friend?

I watched my best friend die in a horrific accident when I was eighteen years old. Thirty-something years later, I can still feel the pain of seeing Jonathon lying there waiting for the ambulance to arrive, the agony of telling his parents what happened, and ultimately, the hurt of losing a friend who had so much life to live.

I'm certain that experience is driving this.

Mike and I haven't talked about the risks, even though they are real—and I'm not sure why.

Yesterday, I asked Mike to send me Michelle's number.

He looked at me and rolled his eyes.

He didn't ask for Sue's number, but I sent it anyway.

FORTY-THREE

Ride Day Twenty

THE PIG TRAIL

The Embassy Suites was the total package. Everything from the oversized bath towels to made-to-order omelets made it the best accommodations of the trip.

I asked Mike what he thought about staying another night so we could be rested when we get home. He didn't buy it.

"You'll be staying by yourself."

Saying Goodbye

After the best breakfast of the trip, we loaded up. On the way out, I spoke with the Business Office Manager and told her how much I enjoyed the facilities. She was surprised, yet pleased, that I made an effort to find her. Excellence needs to be recognized.

We loaded our bikes, exited the parking lot, and turned left onto I-40 heading east a few blocks away. Tulsa traffic wasn't bad, and we were making good time in no time.

Today was supposed to be simple, with a slight detour to ride a final top ten road. Unfortunately, we had an "event" that made it far from boring. More on that later.

Arkansas

The ride on I-40 seemed bland. No mountains, no turquoise lakes, no big skies. It was hot, and I preferred to stay moving.

One hundred miles later, I called for a photo stop to capture the sign welcoming us to Arkansas (rule broken). Then in another 40 miles, we exited onto Highway 23 near White Oak and found a spot for gas and a snack. A sign on the door read:

"Red Hog Deli: Homemade Fudge, Chicken on a Stick, Crawfish Boudin, Homemade Fried Pies, and Frog Legs."

Hum, I thought. What should I try first? We chose none of the above. Instead, we ate a normal snack and enjoyed a few minutes of inside cool. Then we suited up and continued on Highway 23 heading north toward our last detour to ride a twisty road.

The Pig Trail

The Pig Trail Scenic Byway is a 19-mile stretch of Highway 23 that runs through the Ozark National Forest.

It's considered by many to be a top ten road for motorcyclists.

We pulled over and took a picture of the sign signaling we had arrived. A yellow and white road sign warned:

"VERY CROOKED AND STEEP."

We continued anyway.

Once we hit the curves, Mike took off.

Before he got out of range, I called out in my helmet.

"If you crash this close to home, I'm going to be pissed!"

I'm confident he rolled his eyes inside his helmet.

A few seconds later, my helmet beeped.

We were close to the finish line, and I didn't want the biggest memory of the trip to be that one of us crashed in Arkansas.

Just like I had done before, I coached myself through it.

"Take it easy, keep your head level, look through the curves."

Every couple of miles, Mike slowed and let me catch up.

I continued to ride at my own pace.

Several miles later, we stopped at Turner Bend country store. When we went inside, the ladies who worked there told us that the rest of the route was closed due to road construction.

Mike and I were not upset.

I convinced myself that the second half of the Pig Trail was probably like the half we had just ridden.

That seemed good enough.

While there, Mike asked for directions to the Oark Cafe, an old country store that riders in forums say is a must-stop.

We thanked them for the info and continued north. One mile later, we turned right onto Highway 215 heading east.

Highway 215 had lots of curves—and we enjoyed every one.

Fifteen miles later, we pulled up to the Oark Cafe.

Talk about character—this place has it. I wasn't hungry, but we went inside and bought a snack anyway to support the business. Established in 1890, the Oark Cafe seemed even more authentic and real than Crane's Country Store did on Ride Day Two.

I got a MoonPie and Sun Drop to make it true southern.

Our bikes were the only vehicles outside, so I ran out to take photos before that had a chance to change. The setting screamed for black-and-white. I snapped 51 pictures to capture the moment. Old country stores are treasures.

I didn't want to leave.

We geared back up, synced our helmet headsets—a necessary step after every stop—then pulled out.

We backtracked a few miles and turned left onto Highway 103 heading south. Twenty miles later, we connected back with I-40 in Clarksville, Arkansas and continued southeast.

The Event

According to signs, we were 100 miles from our final destination for the evening, Little Rock, Arkansas, and we had plenty of gas to make it without stopping. This should be easy, I thought.

Near Conway, Arkansas traffic picked up to rush-hour levels. Cars and trucks were all around us. We came up on an 18-wheeler that was going slower than we wanted, so Mike pulled into the left lane to pass.

That's when it happened.

When Mike got even with the rear tires on the trailer, I heard a huge explosion. For an instant, I thought Mike's engine had blown or that he had hit something.

Mike said something in his helmet, but I couldn't understand him. A fraction of a second later, I realized what had happened. A left-rear trailer tire on the 18-wheeler had exploded.

I figured this out when I saw pieces of rubber flying at me.

My first instinct was to brake hard. This would at least make the crash less severe. But I knew cars were all around me and that being run over wouldn't feel good.

I decided my best option was to drive through it.

Instead of one large chunk, the tire exploded into hundreds of smaller pieces. Worse than that, a large (two feet long) metal piece had come off in the explosion and was tumbling toward me.

That's the piece I'm going to avoid, I thought.

I swerved to the left and dodged the metal piece, but I ran over some of the smaller pieces of rubber. About the time I made it past the debris field, Mike called out.

"Are you alright?!"

"Yes. Are you?"

Seconds later, the reality of the moment hit me.

My heart raced.

I started breathing heavily and realized that Mike and I could have crashed—maybe *should* have crashed.

Catching my breath wasn't easy. My GS said it was 102 degrees outside my gear. It was even hotter inside.

The truck driver was shaken too. He pulled into the right lane to stop. As I passed, he looked at me and waved as though to say he was sorry. It wasn't his fault. I think I nodded back.

Mike and I didn't stop, but we did check for accidents.

I suppose the condition of our drawers is personal.

Mike wouldn't want me telling his little secret.

Final Destination

We made it to our spot for the evening, the Holiday Inn Express in Little Rock, Arkansas without further incidents.

The exploding tire was bad enough, but the mess of the afternoon ride was worse. Mike and I agree that the worst drivers we've encountered so far are in Arkansas. *Not even close.*

One lady texting crossed into my lane without noticing me.

Another changed lanes and almost hit Mike.

We are blessed to be alive.

Today wasn't a long ride day, but I'm happy it's over. It felt like my brain was cooking in my helmet.

Summer heat down South is real.

After we checked in, we had a team meeting and decided that it was probably time to transition back to normal food.

Jason's Deli (across a four-lane road) got the nod.

I was a little nervous crossing the busy road.

"It would suck to make it this far and die walking to dinner."

Mike agreed.

We made it across fine, got our money's worth at the salad bar, and crossed back to our hotel without any problems.

As I write this, I'm nervous about what the salad might do to me. My insides are either happy or in shock.

Only time will tell.

Lord willing, we *should* arrive back home tomorrow.

Mike's Point of View

I don't like riding near 18-wheelers. Those trucks are a death trap to motorcyclists. I always pass them as quickly as possible.

We were near Conway, Arkansas when it happened.

The afternoon heat was intense, and my brain was roasting in my helmet. I ran up on an 18-wheeler going slower than I wanted, so I eased to the left lane and began to pass.

As I reached the trailer's rear wheels, I felt a concussion—like someone had fired a shotgun.

I'm certain I yelled into my headset, but I don't recall what. I looked at the truck to my right and saw the rear tire disintegrating.

I rolled the throttle back and thought:

David is in the shrapnel trail!

A few seconds later, I looked back and saw that David was still upright and the truck was pulling off.

We were both shaken.

Final Thoughts

The tire explosion was a good wake-up call. We're close to making it back home, and I'm starting to feel too comfortable. We talked at dinner and agreed we should dial it back a notch tomorrow.

When we got back to the hotel after dinner, I started writing this ride report. Two minutes later, I looked over, and Mike was sitting in the chair asleep.

We are both exhausted.

That, and our bodies are in shock from the salad.

States Traveled: Oklahoma and Arkansas
Miles Ridden: 298.5

Reflections One Year Later

David's Thoughts

I don't recall much about the Pig Trail. Like the Million Dollar Highway, I was so focused on good riding that I missed most of it.

That's okay. It's not that far from home.

We downplayed the tire explosion to our wives in my original daily summary. I added more details above.

We were both shaken by the experience.

I stand by my observation that Arkansas had the worst drivers. We almost died there several times.

Mike's Thoughts

If you're ever riding in Northeast Arkansas, riding the Pig Trail and visiting the Oark Cafe is a must. Grab a burger and a piece of pie. Folks have been eating there for more than 100 years.

Hello Arkansas

The Pig Trail

It Sure Was

Mike Crashed

Oark Cafe — One of My Favorite Photos on Trip

FORTY-FOUR

Ride Day Twenty-One

SWEET HOME ALABAMA

TUESDAY
LITTLE ROCK, ARKANSAS TO HUNTSVILLE, ALABAMA

The Holiday Inn Express was old just like the one in Green River, Utah. I grabbed a cinnamon roll but didn't eat it.

Maybe the salad from last night was speaking to me.

While we were going through our morning routine, Mike said, "Dave, we don't have to be in a hurry this morning."

What?

Did Mike (a.k.a. The Timeline Enforcer) fall out of bed during the night and bang his head?

This isn't the Mike I just rode to Alaska with.

Mike and I knew this morning was our last, but we didn't talk about it. Instead, we were mostly silent.

I loaded my side bags for the last time (everything fits so nicely since I mailed extras home in Montana) and took a few pictures of how I packed them in case I wanted to remember.

We put on our riding gear, synced our helmet headsets, and caught I-40 heading east a mile or so down the road.

Tennessee and Mississippi

About 120 miles later, markers signaled we were near the state line. We looked for a sign welcoming us but never found one.

That was okay. The Mississippi River separates Arkansas from Tennessee at this location. I don't think we would have stopped in the middle of a bridge. We have our safety limits.

We meandered our way through Memphis, Tennessee just fine (I-40 to I-55 to I-240 to Highway 385) to the familiar road that goes in the direction of home, Highway 72.

A short time later, we stopped for gas one last time.

We ate lunch at McAlister's in Corinth, Mississippi. While we were eating, one of us said out loud what we were both thinking to ourselves.

This is our last meal on this adventure.

I quickly changed the subject to keep from getting emotional.

The entire day was filled with a day of lasts—our last morning routine, our last gas stop, our last meal.

When we approached our bikes after lunch (for the last time), I couldn't help but notice how clean Mike's screen was in comparison to mine. He cleaned his on most days, and I hadn't cleaned mine since we left Alabama.

"Dave, you want to use some of my spray?"

"Nope. I like that my GS has mud on it from Alaska."

Sweet Home Alabama

When we got close to the Alabama line, I asked Mike to help me look for the state sign. Forty miles from lunch, we found it.

Dark pink crepe myrtles framed the old stone perfectly.

This was the most picturesque state marker of the entire trip, and I'm not just saying that because I call Alabama home.

On the next stretch of asphalt, I couldn't help but compare the landscape to what we had seen on the way to Alaska and back.

I figured Alabama would look less spectacular.

But it was just the opposite. Alabama looked amazing.

The sky was a deep blue, and scattered white clouds appeared magically suspended below. Cotton and soybeans fields framed the foreground.

I told Mike we needed to pull over one last time.

He agreed—and we did.

Normal looked so good.

Riding Solo

One hour later, Mike and I parted ways in Huntsville, Alabama. Mike continued east on I-565 toward his home, and I exited north toward mine. Like guys do, we kept goodbye short.

More than a few words would have choked me up.

For the first time in 21 days, I was now riding solo.

My mind was racing with gratitude.

I'm blessed to have family and friends who care about me.

Blessed to have a job that puts food on the table.

And blessed to have just ridden a motorcycle from Alabama to Alaska and back with a guy I can still call my best friend.

When I turned into my neighborhood, it felt comfortable—yet unfamiliar. I felt like a different person than I did when I left.

Somehow, I knew in my heart that I'd never be able to explain in words what just happened—even to the ones I love the most.

I turned the corner onto my street and rolled back the throttle hard one last time. The front-wheel gently pulled off the ground.

My family (along with my son's best friend, Will) was standing in my front yard holding handmade posters welcoming me home.

I teared up inside my helmet.

I turned into my driveway and came to a complete stop, being extra careful not to drop her in front of everyone.

I took off my helmet for the last time.

I hugged my family like I hadn't seen them in 21 days.

My life looked better than it did when I left. Probably because for the first time in a really long time—I took the time to notice.

It's amazing what riding to Alaska can teach a guy.

States Traveled: Arkansas, Tennessee, Mississippi, and Alabama
Miles Ridden: 343.5

Reflections One Year Later

MIKE'S THOUGHTS

The ride from Little Rock to Huntsville was depressing.

Seeing something new every day had become addictive.

I don't remember much about our last day—just eating lunch in Corinth, Mississippi, and David calling for a final photo stop to capture one of Alabama's many cotton fields.

Our expedition ended as quickly as it began.

It was everything I had imagined and more.

I was glad to be back with my wife and kids, but I was sad that tomorrow my life would be back to normal—waking up, going to work, and stepping through the motions of my existence.

Our Last Ride Day Sign — Day Twenty-One

Packing Up for the Last Time

Hello Mississippi

Our Last Meal — in Corinth, Mississippi

Hello Alabama — Again

A Beautiful Alabama Afternoon

Signs from My Family

One BIG DREAM Completed!

And finally, my favorite photo of the entire trip …

My Welcome Home! — David, Drew, Maddie, Will, and Sue

FORTY-FIVE

Final Thoughts

FIVE YEARS LATER

B efore we part ways, I want to THANK YOU.
I know you have a limited amount of time (we all do),
and I'm honored that you followed along.

I didn't set out to find myself on this adventure, but it's hard to
ride a motorcycle from Alabama to Alaska and back without being
affected by the experience—and I was.

The high points of the trip had little to do with the destination. Rather it was the journey that stands out the most.

I enjoyed seeing the unexpected show up in the expected.

I enjoyed living on a motorcycle for 21 days straight.

I enjoyed meeting people along the way.

What We Did Wrong

In the end, we made more than a few mistakes.

I changed motorcycles and got new gear right before we left.

We didn't take an overnight test ride to flush things out.

We took too long at tourist stops.

We ate too many carbs and not enough salads.

We didn't exercise a single time.

And I did it all without a tank bag.

I'm certain most everyone who has done a long-distance ride could compile a list of mistakes. Yes, we made mistakes—but we still made it. I think I liked it better that way.

What We Did Right

Even though we didn't do everything perfectly, the adventure was a success—in part because we flexed with the obstacles presented.

Adversity was the thing I looked forward to the most. I wanted my endurance to be tested. I wanted to face challenges that forced us to adjust. I wanted to be surprised by something big.

And when it happened, we overcame each obstacle with confidence and calm. We found better rain gear when we needed to. We cut the ride day short when Mike struggled with hypothermia. We made a quick getaway when Mike gave Dennis the digital path to my ride reports.

Mike replanned the trip several times over—beginning when his title problem forced us to delay our departure date.

I replaced a headlight at a campground in Canada.

We Got Along and Got Over Issues Fast

If I wanted to stop for a photo, Mike was always happy to. He didn't pout like I was messing up his schedule. When Mike disappeared into the mountain creek in Canada, I just smiled because I knew that was important to him.

We didn't bicker for the sake of being right. We sensed when the other guy was happy, tired, or frustrated and adjusted accordingly. We put the needs of each other ahead of our own.

We Got a Jump on the Day

On most mornings, we left early and knocked out 100 miles before our first stop, and another 100 miles before lunch.

Having 200 miles behind us so early in the day was huge.

We always topped off our fuel tanks before we ended our day. This made our mornings more productive.

We Connected with People

I never envisioned that meeting people along the way would be such a big part of our adventure. Mike and I were more open to engaging with people than in our normal lives.

Every person had a story, and I longed to hear it.

It was unexpected—incredible.

One Mile at a Time

There were moments along the way when I didn't think I could make it to the end of the day, and a mile at the time was the most I could get my mind around.

So that's what I focused on—the next mile.

It's the same in life—one day at a time is always good enough.

On the way back from Alaska, I spent hours thinking inside my helmet, trying to decide how I should answer the question:

"Tell me about your trip to Alaska."

Do I focus on the route?

Do I give details of each day?

Or do I tell them it was awesome and leave it at that?

I never perfected my answer and usually start by saying,

"It's a long way from Alabama to Alaska—a very long way."

This at least gets a smile.

Memories

When I wasn't consumed with the mechanics of riding, I focused on the beauty around me and thought about my life.

At nearly every stop, I pulled out a folded piece of paper from my back pocket and scribbled out my thoughts and ideas. *Most were incorporated into this book.*

Our adventure to Alaska is something I'll cherish for the rest of my life. I'll remember the amazing beauty that surrounded us. I'll remember the excitement of making it—and the overwhelming feeling of knowing we were still only halfway to home.

I'll remember the hot showers after riding in the cold, and the cold showers after riding in the heat. I'll remember the sights along the way that made me pause and notice. I'll remember the total joy (and emptiness) I felt when we got close to home.

But more than anything, I'll remember how people treated us and made us feel like we were doing something special.

The South

Some say that people in the South are friendlier.

I'm not so sure that's true.

Where I live, people rush around from one thing to the next. I rarely speak to strangers, and strangers rarely speak to me. This trip showed me that people are friendly all the way to Alaska and back.

I'm blessed to have shared this experience with a friend. Mike and I never fussed for longer than it took to see the next amazing thing. In 8,058 miles, I didn't uncover anything disturbing about Mike, and I hope he didn't discover anything surprising about me.

As far as I'm concerned, this trip strengthened our friendship.

Mike, if I could have chosen anyone in the world to ride to Alaska and back with, it would have been you.

Closing

When I got home, normal life came faster than I wanted it to. The uniqueness of our adventure was quickly forgotten by my friends and family—and the questions faded fast.

Years later, people rarely ask me about my journey, and I never bring it up. But that's okay. I didn't do it to impress anyone.

The adventure would mean the same if I hadn't told a soul.

Looking back, the low points on the trip were always followed by high points. An argument in downtown St. Louis was followed by a special visit to Crane's Country Store. A bad camping experience in Montana was followed by a majestic desert ride in Utah. A 680-mile ride through the blistering heat in Kansas was followed by a refreshing stay at the Embassy Suites.

I've found this to be true in my normal life too. High points are almost always just around the corner from low points.

My parents taught me this:

"Just make it till morning, and everything will seem better."

They were right.

What took us 21 days to experience in real-time took me more than five years to put into words. Writing this book has allowed me to relive it at a pace I can absorb.

For this, I am thankful.

Absence makes the heart grow fonder. Twenty-one days later, my life in Alabama seemed better than it did when I left.

Sometimes things outside of our comfort zone have a way of resetting our perspective. This adventure did this for me. My house seemed bigger, my wife more gorgeous, my dogs friendlier, my kids kinder, my friends funnier—and my work more rewarding.

Mike said it best when we were at Chief Mountain.

"Dave, I don't have the vocabulary to describe this."

He was right.

Words can't fully describe what we experienced.

In the end, questions about our trip may have faded, but the lessons of the adventure will live with me forever. Riding a motorcycle to Alaska made the world feel smaller—in a good way.

Mike and I did something that few people get to do.

We completed a DREAM RIDE of a LIFETIME.

I'm grateful for the opportunity to do it.

I'm blessed to have a friend to share it with.

I'm thrilled that we did it.

And at fifty-something, I'm wise enough to realize that I have a limited number of these trips left in me. This makes the one I just went on a little extra special.

It's a long way from Huntsville, Alabama to Hyder, Alaska.
I will cherish every single mile for the rest of my life!

FORTY-SIX

Motorcycle Smarts Quick Tips
Newsletter

I realize that not everyone who reads this book rides. But if you do, take action now.

The 'Motorcycle Smarts' Quick Tips Newsletter is where I share my best riding tips (some of which didn't make it into any of my books) and keep you informed about what's next. Sign up at the link below. Unsubscribe at any time.
motorcyclesmarts.com/tips

"Motorcycle Smarts" Quick Tips Newsletter

Free weekly riding tips you can consume in less than 3 minutes— delivered to your inbox for you to use and share with others.

motorcyclesmarts.com/tips

You're not doing everything you can to keep from crashing until you're signed up.

Appendix

BONUS MATERIAL

This section gives a behind-the-scenes look into the trip statistics, and Mike and I answer your frequently asked questions.

But before we get to that—I have a personal challenge for you.

FORTY-SEVEN

My Final Challenge

DARE TO DREAM

For the longest, one of my dreams was to ride somewhere big. But instead of taking action, I made excuses.

I don't have enough money.

My family needs me at home.

My work can't make it without me for that long.

One year ago, that changed. I said no to fear and yes to myself. I fulfilled one of my BIG DREAMS.

I rode a motorcycle to Alaska and back.

WHAT DO YOU DREAM OF DOING BUT HAVEN'T?

Looking back, my excuses seem so lame. I still have enough money to send my kids to college. I still have a job. And my family did just fine while I was gone. Sure, my BIG DREAM took time and money, but I don't regret a single moment or dime spent.

WHAT EXCUSES ARE GETTING IN YOUR WAY?

My Personal Challenge

If you're okay with it, I'd like to help you find your BIG DREAM.

If you're not, skip ahead to the next chapter.

Find a quiet place.

Grab your favorite beverage.

Let your mind go free.

You'll need a couple of sheets of paper and a pen.

When you're ready, proceed with the steps below.

Step #1: Make a list of your BIG DREAMS.

What have you dreamed of doing but haven't?

Most people know the answer(s) to this question instantly. But some might need time to uncover them. It's fine to go crazy here.

Don't hold back.

If you have more than one BIG DREAM, that's fine.

Maybe your BIG DREAM is to run a marathon, restore an old car, or hike the Appalachian Trail. Maybe it's to backpack across Europe—or spend a month at the beach.

Go ahead and fill up the page with ideas if you'd like.

We'll process through them next.

Step #2: Select one BIG DREAM.

Take some time to look through your list of BIG DREAMS.

Is there one that excites you the most?

Let your mind go. When you find the "one," circle it.

If you're struggling to select just one, read your list out loud. The one that makes you smile the most is the one to circle.

That's your BIG DREAM.

Step #3: Make a list of what's needed.

Make a list of what you need to complete your BIG DREAM.
What resources (money, time, health, desire) do you need?
Be specific. Be honest.

Step #4: Evaluate your current situation.

Do you have what you need (money, time, health, desire)?
As an example, let's say your BIG DREAM is to hike part of the Appalachian Trail.
How much will it cost (new gear, food, lodging)?
How long will it take (travel there, the hike, travel back)?
Do you have enough time away from work?
Can you be away from home?
Are you in good enough health to complete it?
How strong is your desire to make it happen?
What are you willing to do to make it happen?

Step #5: Define your roadblocks.

Make a list of reasons why you can't do your BIG DREAM.
Be specific. Be honest. Be real.

Step #6: Develop a path forward.

Now, look at your list of roadblocks from Step #5 and ask yourself:
What would need to happen for my DREAM to be a reality?
Again, be honest. This won't work if you're not.

Step #7: Share your BIG DREAM.

Now's the time to talk to your family and boss.

Tell them you don't have everything planned out but that you want to take time away to live out one of your BIG DREAMS.

My wife wasn't all that excited when I told her I wanted to ride my motorcycle to Alaska. But she warmed up to the idea when she saw how important it was to me.

Now is the time to live your BIG DREAM.

At one point, riding a motorcycle to Alaska seemed impossible.

Now, I regret putting it off for so long.

Ultimately, I had everything I needed to make it.

You probably do too.

FORTY-EIGHT

Trip Statistics

THE DATA

T he ride from Huntsville to Hyder was 3,787 miles.
It took us nine days (not including the BMW rally).
The ride back was 4,271 miles and took us ten days.
Over the 19 ride days, we averaged 424 miles per day.
In total, we rode 8,058 miles and averaged 59 mph (while we were moving) and 41 mph (if you include idling time).
Mike's GPS calculated that for us.
Total time in the seat was 196 hours—about ten hours a day.
We stopped for gas 42 times.

Accommodations

We camped five nights and stayed in hotels the rest. The most expensive ($200/night) was the Hampton Inn in Idaho Falls. The least expensive ($75/night) was the Bighorn Hotel in Radium Hot Springs. A close second was the Sealaska in Hyder ($79/night).

The hotel with the worst value was the Super 8 in Durango ($160/night), and the hotel with the best value, by far, was the Embassy Suites in Tulsa ($104/night).

Cost

Riding a motorcycle to Alaska wasn't cheap.

The trip cost me about $222 a day. I had several big purchases that I included in the total cost.

The Numbers

Hotels (15 nights) = $2,056 (total) = $1,028 each
    Gas (8,058 miles at 40 mpg and $3.09/gallon) = $622 each
    Camping (5 nights) = $187 (total) = $94 each
    Food and snacks = $30/day = $630 each
    Miscellaneous = not included
    Riding gear = $0 (I needed anyway)
    Phone (Canadian plan) = $40
    Camping gear = $500 for me
    Tires = $400 for me
    Oil change = $50 for me
    BMW rally = $60 each
    Headlamp = $10
    Helmet headsets = $227 each
    Motorcycle depreciation* = $1,000 (estimated)
    Time away from work = not included
    Time away from family = not included

Total Cost for me = $4,661.00

Note: Motorcycle deprecation costs are real and shouldn't be ignored. My motorcycle is worth at least $1,000 less with an additional 8,000 miles on it.

This trip wasn't cheap, but it was worth it.

We camped fewer nights than we originally planned because of the weather. That made the trip about $300 more for each of us.

It's also worth noting here that living my normal life at home during the 21 days would have cost money (food and gas).

More Facts

Our longest ride day was 803 miles. Our shortest was 160.

Mike and I both averaged about 40 mpg.

Mike's top speed (captured by his GPS) was 93 mph.

My top speed (estimated by me) was over 100 mph.

I got stuck passing slow cars and needed to catch up.

Mike never dropped his bike. I dropped mine once.

Neither of us stalled out or started in any gear other than first gear (that we're willing to admit—cough, cough).

Mike added oil a couple of times because his GS was leaking.

I never cracked open the oil fill plug on my GS.

We saw several bears in Canada, a handful of bighorn sheep in Radium Hot Springs, several deer in Canada and Colorado, thousands of salmon in Alaska, hundreds of chipmunks in Colorado, eagles in Alaska and Canada, a herd of bison in Wyoming—and more senior citizens watching salmon swim than I was expecting.

We ate more burgers and fewer salads than I realized in real-time. We argued very little, became frustrated hardly ever, and got lost not once. We at least knew where we were with Mike's GPS.

We rode in the rain more than either of us wanted. And one of us nearly died of hypothermia (slight exaggeration) in Montana.

Gas stations in Canada are way too far apart.

Gas stations in the western U.S. are a bit too far apart.

Gas stations in the southeastern U.S. are too close together.

Mike cleaned his windscreen on most days.
   I cleaned mine zero times in 21 days.
   One year later, I still haven't cleaned it.

I sort of like that the muck on my windscreen came from my
   DREAM RIDE to ALASKA.

FORTY-NINE

Frequently Asked Questions

MIKE AND I ANSWER YOUR QUESTIONS

M ike and I have been asked a lot of questions. Here are our responses to nine of the most frequently asked ones.

1. What were your biggest challenges?

DAVID: I didn't share this in the daily ride reports, but one of the things I struggled with the most was falling asleep.

I'm sure my diet didn't help.

At one point, I told Mike that I needed to pull over. We found a shady spot under a large tree, and I laid my head over the tank and took a power nap.

I was exhausted.

I also struggled with the mental and physical requirements of having to ride a long way every day. On most days, there simply wasn't enough time between parking our bikes for the evening and suiting up again the next morning.

I longed for more margin, but there wasn't any. The only way to get from Alabama to Alaska (and back) in 21 days is to go hard.

MIKE: Before we left, I thought my biggest challenge would be whether I could ride 400+ miles every day for three weeks.

Once we made it to Billings, I knew I could do it.

I never thought of the ride as hard. I enjoyed every day. Were there difficult moments? Sure. The rain and cold were tough, and the 100-degree heat was like riding in a clothes dryer.

My big challenge came on Ride Day Six when we got caught in the Lewis and Clark National Forest in the rain and cold.

I was close to hypothermia.

2. What were your favorite roads?

DAVID: That's a hard question to answer, so I'm going to describe the spurts that come to my mind first.

Beartooth Highway was incredible. The sky was clear, and I felt refreshed because we didn't ride the day before. The switchbacks were great.

Beartooth Highway exceeded my expectations.

I also enjoyed the ride up to Salmon Glacier in Hyder, Alaska. The road was washed out—just enough to be fun—and the views got better and better as we climbed.

It seemed so perfect it almost didn't feel real.

I also enjoyed the ride from Provo, Utah to Green River, Utah. The desert scenery was unexpected and different than anything I had ever seen. It was insanely hot, but that didn't matter.

We were in a special place.

The ride to Pikes Peak was another highlight. I expected less and got more. The rain passed, the clouds cleared, and we were left with a breathtaking view of Colorado.

MIKE: I wish I could say the Million Dollar Highway, but I don't remember much more than yellow road stripes.

3. If you could relive one day, which would it be?

DAVID: Narrowing it to one day is tough, but I think I'd redo our day exploring Alaska.

Our pace was relaxed, and there was a warmth that encompassed the entire day. Hyder was more than I expected.

Salmon Glacier was spectacular.

Meeting friends seemed natural.

Alaska was everything I'd hoped for and more.

MIKE: Kind of a tough question, but I think I'd redo the day we rode from Durango to Colorado Springs.

It was a beautiful day to ride. We saw some of the best parts of southern and central Colorado, and we rode Pikes Peak.

Riding Pikes Peak was a nice surprise. The twisted road up and down was sensory overload. I was expecting to smell the mountain air and the hint of pine needles, but I smelled hot brakes.

Still, that's the day I would do over.

4. What would you do differently?

MIKE: I would plan for more days. We averaged almost 425 miles per day. That was too far, considering the roads we were riding.

We needed more time to absorb the views and meet people.

5. What surprised you the most?

DAVID: People surprised me the most.

I had no expectations of meeting anyone on this adventure. Sure, I figured we'd strike up conversations with fellow riders at the BMW rally in Billings, but to my surprise, people struck up conversations with *us* all along the way.

Strangers approached us at gas stations, while we were eating, when we were pulled over to take photos. They seemed excited for us when we told them what we were doing.

How cool is that?

People exceeded my expectations—all the way there and back.

MIKE: I was surprised David didn't complain about the heat.

David has a limited operating temperature, and we way more than exceeded it. But he took it all in stride.

6. What area would you most like to explore again?

DAVID: I want to explore southern Colorado again.

On our ride to Colorado Springs, I got the sense we only saw a portion of what this part of Colorado had to offer. Pikes Peak was the exclamation point on a wonderful day.

MIKE: I had to cut our itinerary short to make up for the days we were delayed leaving. I deleted Lolo Pass in Idaho (painful), and we barely saw British Columbia.

I want to explore both.

I also want to go back to Colorado. Colorado has thousands of miles of dirt roads, and I need to ride at least a few of them.

7. Was it easier or harder than you thought it would be?

DAVID: Parts were easier, and parts were harder.

One year later, I'd say it was easier—mainly because my mind doesn't remember the tough parts as clearly as it does the easy.

I remember how great riding Beartooth Highway was, but I don't remember so much that it was cold when we did.

I remember crossing into Alaska, but I don't remember quite as much that it was raining, and we were both exhausted.

My mind has a funny way of remembering things. It remembers the good parts of my life more clearly—and the bad parts as a means to be thankful for the good.

At least some of the time.

MIKE: I never thought about the trip as being easy or hard.

I worked on the route for almost a year. I knew we were in for a long ride. I knew I'd be tired—and I was. Since the route was preplanned, we didn't have to plan as much once we left.

We just got on our bikes and rode. That part was easy.

8. What are your impressions of the BMW R1200GS Adventure?

DAVID: To be honest, I didn't expect the GS to be perfect.

On paper, the boxer engine seemed old-school and outdated. I figured two big pistons couldn't be as good as four smaller ones.

I was wrong.

The engine has more power and torque than I expected, and it doesn't need to spin very fast to make it.

Off-the-line acceleration is very impressive.

She pulls hard to 70 mph, then a little less hard to 100.

Passing power is good, but I sometimes wished for a little more giddy-up when we passed cars going above 60 mph.

9. Any final advice?

DAVID: Don't prepare so much that you freak out when things don't go as planned—because sometimes they won't.

I believe that preparation is vital in most situations. But on our adventure, no amount of planning could have prevented the unexpected—and it will be the same for yours.

My second piece of advice is to manage your expectations.

The weather won't be perfect, and the famous place where you planned to eat might be closed. The Million Dollar Highway was a total bust because the weather was horrendous.

That's all part of the adventure.

MIKE: Make the trip about the journey and not the destination.

Don't over-plan, be flexible, and expect the unexpected.

The destination is only a direction. If you only make it halfway, that's okay. It gives you a reason to go again.

FIFTY

The Title for This Book

Three years after we got back from Alaska, Mike and I were on another adventure—this time riding on back roads and forest roads from Virginia to New York.

I was in the final stages of editing this book, but I was struggling for the perfect title.

We had stopped in Cedar Run, Pennsylvania for a snack when a gentleman walked up and noticed my Alabama tag.

"Are you on your dream ride of a lifetime—or is this something you do every year?"

After a brief pause, I smiled and said:

"The guy over there (pointing to Mike) and I rode our motorcycles to Alaska three years ago."

"That was my DREAM RIDE of a lifetime."

FIFTY-ONE

Good Leader and Good Follower

A TIME TO LEAD AND A TIME TO FOLLOW

M ike was in charge of navigating our adventure. He planned the route each day, loaded the maps into his GPS, and led the way for most of the 8,058 miles.

I think Mike enjoyed doing the planning.

I know I enjoyed not having to.

I didn't know what was around the next corner. I didn't know how many miles we were going on our long days—not because Mike didn't want me to know, but because I didn't want to know.

I wanted to focus on the now, the next turn, the next mile, and I wanted to have space in my head to absorb what I was seeing.

Mike was a good leader.

And I did my best to be a good follower.

Mike invested tons of time researching the path for our trip. The last thing he deserved was a backseat driver who questioned everything. I never asked,

"Why did we go this way instead of that?" or …

"Did you think about going through [blank]?"

My Responsibilities

I was in charge of documenting our trip.

I evaluated every pull-off and weighed its value before I called for a photo stop. I wrote daily summaries and posted them online. I took methodical notes that I used to write this book.

I did my best to be a good leader.

And Mike extended the same courtesy to me.

He never complained when I called for photo stops on interstates—even though it violated one of our rules.

He never said, "But we just stopped a mile ago."

He never nitpicked my daily ride reports.

He said I could publish this book without him reading it first —even though I gave him a proof copy and asked for his inputs.

He replied with a handful of road number corrections.

Mike was a good follower.

Final Thoughts

In the end, I think it worked better because we split the duties.

We both did what we were supposed to do (good leader), and we didn't second-guess the other guy (good follower).

The trip worked better because we did it this way.

Our friendship is stronger because we did it this way.

Would You Help?

I'd like to thank you for purchasing my book.

You could have picked from dozens of other resources, but you took a chance to hear what I had to say. I'm honored.

Before you go, can I ask you for a favor?

If you enjoyed it, would you please write an honest review on Amazon? If this book doesn't consistently receive positive reviews, it won't show up when readers do a search.

I really want this to be a "five-star" quality book.

Thank you for doing this.

P.S. If you've written a review for any of my other books in the 'Motorcycle Smarts' series. Thank you so much!

More Motorcycle Smarts Books

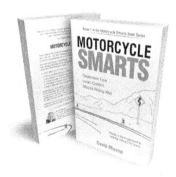

Motorcycle Smarts: Overcome Fear, Learn Control, Master Riding Well

Motorcycle Smarts is the first book in the *Motorcycle Smarts* series. Do you feel *guilty* for wanting to ride a motorcycle?

Do you have a *fear* that overcomes you when you ride?

Do you want to enjoy the *peace of mind* knowing that you're doing everything possible NOT to crash?

Riders crash and die every day in RIDER-INDUCED crashes —and it doesn't have to be this way.

In addition to in-depth discussions about rider fear and how not to crash, *Motorcycle Smarts* tackles important topics like *countersteering, muscle memory,* and *braking*.

It also goes over some of the most important lessons from the Hurt Report and makes a case for riding motorcycles with ABS.

You won't find page-filling discussions about bike rallies and riding gear. Instead, you'll find the most in-depth explanation of lowside and highside crashes that exists anywhere.

Here's what one reader said:

"I've read 'Total Control,' 'Proficient Motorcycling,' and 'Stayin Safe,' but the section in 'Motorcycle Smarts' on lowside and highside crashes is all the difference. David is great at simplifying difficult concepts. I'm definitely passing along this book to my riding friends."

— Dano in San Diego, California

Mastering the art of riding well is about understanding and overcoming *fear*. It's about having the *head knowledge of how your motorcycle works* so you can make it go where you want it to go.

It's about *taking ownership of your riding safety*.

For more information visit:
motorcyclesmarts.com/books

Motorcycle Hacks: Everything My Motorcycle Mentors Taught Me—and More

Motorcycle Hacks is the third book in the *Motorcycle Smarts* series.

In this book, I share some of the riding tips my mentors shared with me when I first started riding. I also tackle tough topics like whether loud pipes really save lives.

This book doesn't cover the lame topics that the most popular motorcycle mega books do to fill pages—like how to select a helmet and get the most out of your first motorcycle rally. Instead, I cover the topics that matter.

Motorcycle Hacks is for anyone who is just thinking about riding—or who has been riding for decades.

Here's what readers have said:

> *"Reading this book felt like I was talking*
> *to David over coffee."*
>
> — Dan in San Diego, California

"Riders who practice the suggestions in 'Motorcycle Hacks' are guaranteed to be less likely to crash. It's nicely illustrated, with important ideas explained clearly and repeatedly. It contains rider wisdom not found in other publications. This book will definitely save lives."

— Mark, Motorcycle Owner and Rider

In this book, I also make a case for Congress to mandate ABS and Electronic Stability Control on all on-street motorcycles—and share three things I think could change the crash data.

"My goal is to help one rider. That's exactly what my motorcycle mentors did for me when I first started riding."

For more information visit:
motorcyclesmarts.com/books

The Motorcycle Mentor Podcast

I started the *Motorcycle Mentor Podcast* to help riders at all levels understand how motorcycles work—and why they crash. You can listen for FREE on iTunes, Stitcher, Overcast, Apple TV, Pocket Casts, Amazon Music, or iHeartRadio.

The podcast has been downloaded more than 250,000 times. *I'm truly honored!*

Here's what listeners are saying ...

"Best motorcycle podcast yet! This is a very well-done podcast with a lot of useful information that might save your life. I've been riding for over seven years now, and I've introduced quite a few people to motorcycle riding over the years. These podcasts are well-researched and well-written. Keep up the good work."

— Mrbeanproduction via iTunes

"A MUST LISTEN for any rider!"

— Brent Boxall via iTunes

"I've been riding for 30+ years and found all of the podcasts that I have listened to thoughtful, informative, and interesting. You have tackled excellent topics in a way as to help all. Please continue."

— Harley/Guzzi Guy via iTunes

"So thankful I found this podcast. David is personable, humble, and knowledgeable."

— NMcClure via iTunes

David Here ...

I'll tell you this upfront. I don't have a radio voice, but I do have the heart of a teacher. I work hard to make each show informative and to the point. If you enjoyed this book, you'd like the podcast.

I strive to make the show a "five-star" quality podcast.

You can learn more about the podcast at:
motorcyclesmarts.com/podcast

About the Author

On Pikes Peak in Colorado

Hi. I'm David: husband, father, engineer, and author.

I like watching sunrises and sunsets, writing at the beach, and collecting hard-to-find bourbons. And I also like motorcycles—even though I didn't buy my first real one until I was forty.

Mike Shell (the other half of this gig) and I met 30 years ago at NASA—the space place.

We've been friends ever since.

In case you're wondering, nothing about this ride changed our friendship. We still eat lunch together on most work days and chat about every topic imaginable—including where we should go on our next big motorcycle adventure.

Mike and I married our wives while we were still young.

I managed to get my college sweetheart to say *yes* over 30 years ago. She's an amazing redheaded southern girl named Sue.

Sue and I have two children (Maddie and Drew).

We also have three dogs (two Shih Tzus and a Great Dane).

Mike married a special lady named Michelle almost 30 years ago. They have three children (Alex, Anna, and Ian)—*and no dogs.*

———

If you've read my other books in this series, you know I'm passionate about the sport. You also know that I strongly believe that ABS and ESC should be federally mandated as standard equipment for all on-street motorcycles.
If someone wants to champion that effort to Congress,
I'd be happy to do what I can to help.
Thanks again for following along.

—David
david@motorcyclesmarts.com
linkedin.com/in/david-mixson/

CPSIA information can be obtained
at www.ICGtesting.com
Printed in the USA
LVHW041301030723
751435LV00004B/34